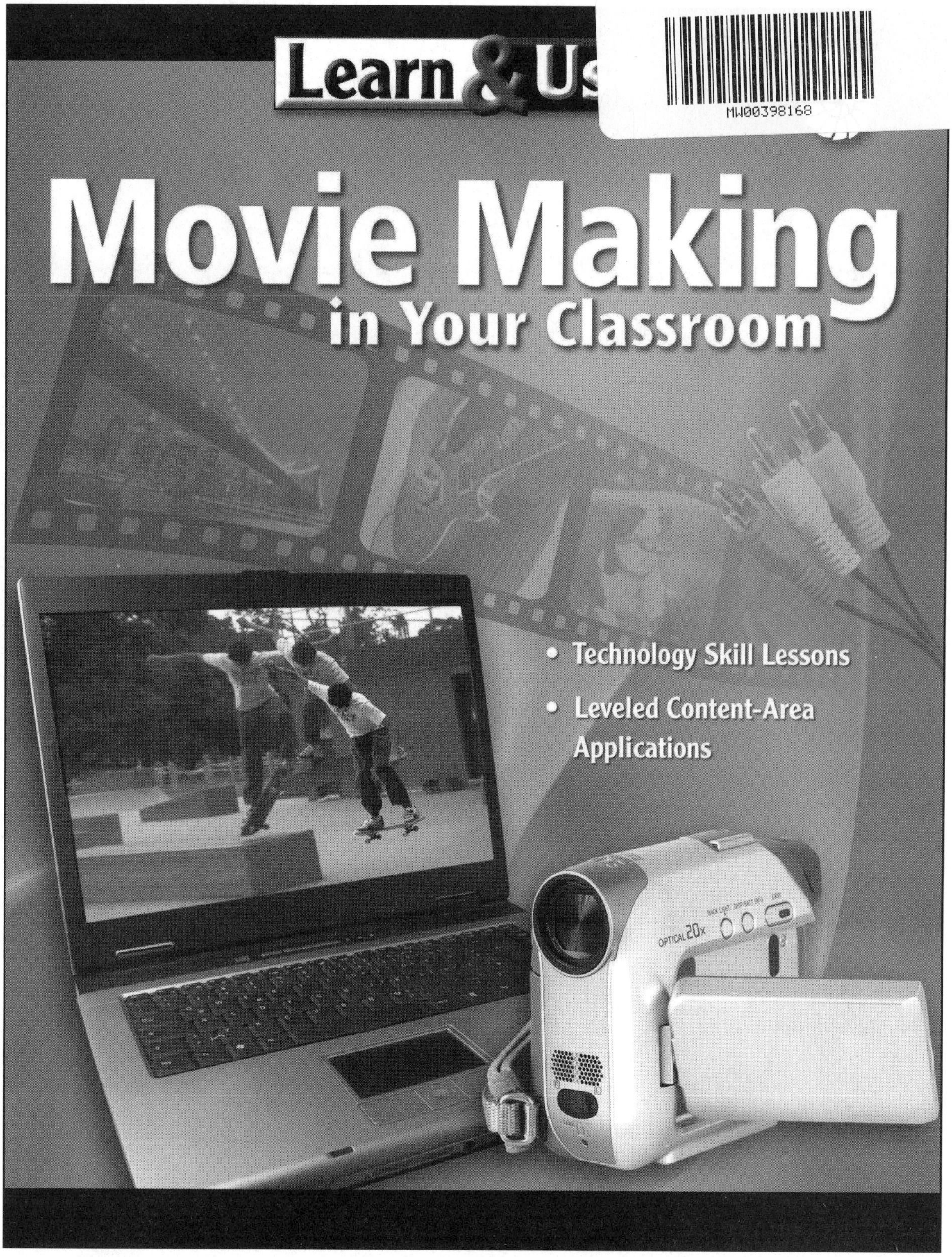

Learn & Us

Movie Making in Your Classroom

- Technology Skill Lessons
- Leveled Content-Area Applications

Author

Patti Englebert

SHELL EDUCATION

Publishing Credits

Contributing Author
Elin Cook, M.Ed.

Editor
Sara Johnson

Associate Editor
Torrey Maloof

Editorial Assistant
Kathryn R. Kiley

Editorial Director
Emily R. Smith, M.A.Ed.

Editor-in-Chief
Sharon Coan, M.S.Ed.

Editorial Manager
Gisela Lee, M.A.

Creative Director
Lee Aucoin

Cover Designer
Lesley Palmer

Print Production Manager
Don Tran

Print Production
Juan Chavolla
Kimberly Weber

Illustration Manager
Timothy J. Bradley

Publisher
Corinne Burton, M.A.Ed.

Shell Education
5301 Oceanus Drive
Huntington Beach, CA 92649-1030
http://www.shelleducation.com
ISBN 978-1-4258-0190-8

Table of Contents

What Research Says About Technology Use in the Classroom

In recent years, technology use in the classroom has become widespread at all grade levels. In fact, a recent study by the U.S. Department of Education found that 75 percent or more of America's students were in schools with access to computers in classrooms or in labs (Mitchell, Bakia, and Yang 2007). Educators face the challenge of preparing students for a world that is becoming more technologically advanced with each passing moment. Therefore, students must learn how to use different forms of technology in the classrooms, and schools must equip their students with the skills and knowledge required to succeed in such an ever-changing world.

Technology use must be taught within an appropriate context—students should be able to make connections between learning about particular topics and knowing how technology can contribute to those learning experiences. Therefore, integrating technology into content-area instruction is a key component to any effective technology program. Simply memorizing the steps needed to complete skills in isolation will not help students see the critical role that technology can play in learning about the real world. *Learn & Use Movie Making in Your Classroom* offers a complete and integrated program—it takes practical and necessary technology skills and introduces them to students within the meaningful context of subject-matter content.

An extensive amount of research has been conducted over the years to determine how important and effective technology instruction is for student performance and achievement. Instructional technology, which includes computers, has been attributed to positive gains such as:

- increasing student achievement
- improving higher-order thinking skills and problem-solving abilities
- enhancing student motivation and engagement
- improving students' abilities to work collaboratively (White, Ringstaff, and Kelley 2002)

Gilbert Valdez, et al. (1999) also found similar signs of improvement, some of which extend beyond student learning. Their research finds that technology can:

- make learning more interactive
- enhance the enjoyment of learning
- individualize the curriculum to match the learner's developmental needs and interests
- capture and store data for informing data-driven decision making
- enhance avenues for collaboration among family members and the school community
- improve methods of accountability and reporting

These benefits highlight the importance of incorporating technology instruction into students' daily lives. However, many educators continue to struggle with finding the time to fully integrate technology. First, teachers have difficulty fitting technology training into their busy schedules. Then, if they do take a class, there is little time to practice what they've learned. Finally, without follow-up and further training, important knowledge is lost (Mitchell, Bakia, and Yang 2007). This book helps teachers start integrating technology into their classrooms by introducing the technology through commonly taught content-area topics.

What Research Says About Technology Use in the Classroom *(cont.)*

Michael Eisenberg and Doug Johnson (1996) argue that "effective integration of information skills has two requirements: 1) the skills must directly relate to the content-area curriculum and to classroom assignments and 2) the skills themselves need to be tied together in a logical and systematic information process model." Therefore, the organization and structure of *Learn & Use Movie Making in Your Classroom* will help students acquire proficiency with both subject-matter content and technology skills. Because the technology skills introduced in this book are organized in a logical and sequential order, students may build on their mastery of each skill as they progress through the lessons and activities. In addition, all skills are taught using topics that are directly related to content-area curriculum, and the lessons themselves are easily modified to fit the unique needs of your classroom curriculum.

The last part of this book focuses on project-based learning and technology. Project-based learning provides an "exciting balance between traditional teaching and technology tools" (Britt, Brasher, and Davenport 2007). The project-based learning section also provides integrated lesson plans and activities. These activities, however, are more broad and open-ended, allowing students to enhance both their problem-solving abilities and their critical-thinking skills as they navigate their own ways toward producing final products. Students learn that using technology can provide them with a variety of choices as they make decisions about their own learning. The Works Cited list for this research is included on page 210.

Digital Movie-Making Skills

The lessons in this book are all written for use with *Movie Maker* and *iMovie* software. *Movie Maker* and *iMovie* are programs used to create movies. This allows users to share information in an organized, visual way with an audience. Students can add effects such as motion, sound, and transitions to enhance their work. These exciting programs provide a motivating and interesting way to input and organize photographs and videos. Directions for using the Macintosh version of this software, *iMovie*, are included on the Teacher Resource CD.

Learn & Use Movie Making in Your Classroom will help guide you through the process of teaching students to use technology in appropriate, meaningful, and engaging ways. It will show students that making movies can be a powerful tool to help them learn about various topics and concepts and that technology can play a significant role in their development as learners.

The 45 lessons in this book are organized by grade level and content area. It is recommended that the five lessons for each content area be taught in succession. The five lessons build on one another and culminate in a completed movie. In kindergarten and first grade, students will need direct teacher guidance to complete the activities. In second grade and above, students should be more self-directed. The grade levels are not included on the student pages so that you can use these assignments off level.

Although a single movie-making skill is emphasized in each lesson, other movie-making skills are presented and integrated in the activities themselves. Therefore, students who complete these activities have multiple opportunities to learn and practice various skills using the movie-making software.

Digital Movie-Making Skills *(cont.)*

The movie-making skills included in this book may be introduced in different ways at different grade levels. Likewise, students in different grade levels may learn and use the same skill at slightly varying degrees of complexity. It is strongly recommended that you review all the lessons (even ones that are not written for the grade(s) you teach) for a particular skill to see which lesson may be the best fit for your students.

Movie-Making Skills in This Book

- Capturing and Importing Images
- Working with Clips
- Working in Storyboard View or Clip Viewer
- Adding Titles and Credits
- Using AutoMovie or Magic iMovie
- Adding Titles Before and After a Clip
- Working with Audio
- Working with Music
- Rearranging Clip Sequences and Deleting Clips
- Selecting a Movie Style
- Filming Techniques
- Using Video Effects
- Recording Narration
- Adjusting Audio Balance
- Producing the Movie
- Saving the Final Movie

How to Use This Book

Learn & Use Movie Making in Your Classroom is comprised of skill-based lesson plans. There are 45 lesson plans grouped under 16 different technology skills, ranging from easy to complex.

Each technology skill is explained with a one-page summary. The *iMovie* and *Movie Maker Vista* versions of these summary pages can be found on the Teacher Resource CD. (See pages 212–215 for a list of filenames.). Keep in mind that there are often several ways to complete a single skill in *Movie Maker* and *iMovie*. Use the software Help menu, as necessary, to clarify any technology steps.

How to Use This Book *(cont.)*

Technology/Content Integration

While the lessons and projects in this book are designed to teach technology skills, the technology skills are integrated with subject matter from the three content areas: mathematics, science, and social studies. Among all the lessons and projects in this book, you will find a fairly even distribution of these topics. This makes the learning experience more authentic for students as they are using real software applications in meaningful and realistic ways. In addition, these teaching ideas give educators a way to motivate students by making core content more interesting and by making technology more applicable to real-world topics.

As you browse the core content topics that are included in this book, keep in mind that most of these lesson plans can be modified or altered to better fit the content that you are currently teaching. For example, a lesson on symmetry can be modified to address another mathematical topic. Likewise, a K–2 lesson on animals could be modified to teach about a more appropriate science topic for grades 6–8. Be creative and think about how the technology skills can be taught with the topics and units of study that you are currently teaching.

Lesson Plans

The lesson plans in this book include all the information that you need to prepare for instruction. Necessary materials are listed and suggestions for teacher preparation are described. Because the technology lessons in the book are also integrated with content-area material, some additional teaching may be required to introduce or review related content with students.

Once you are ready to begin working with *Movie Maker* or *iMovie*, a suggested procedure for teaching the lesson is listed sequentially. At the end of each lesson is a suggestion for extending the lesson for students who are ready to reach further within the content or technology skills.

Some lesson plans specifically mention showing students samples for how to complete the various activities or projects. Student samples for these lessons can be found on the Teacher Resource CD. (See page 211 for a list of sample filenames.)

A list of steps, called Student Directions, can be projected for the whole class or can be distributed to students. This page lists what students will do once they are in front of the computers. Student Directions for Macintosh and *Vista* users can be found on the Teacher Resource CD. (See pages 212–215 for a list of filenames.) Although students will likely have seen the lesson modeled by you before approaching the computers on their own, the Student Directions serve as a reminder for students about what to do to complete the activity.

One popular method of assessing student performance is using a rubric. A rubric is a tool that allows for standardized assessment of student work using specific criteria and a point grading scale. Rubrics are included for all lessons and projects in this book. They include space for both the teacher and the student to assess completed work.

How to Use This Book *(cont.)*

Lesson Plans *(cont.)*

There is also a blank rubric file on the Teacher Resource CD (rubric.pdf). When a project is assessed by both teacher and student, it allows students to be involved in the evaluation process of their own work and makes expectations clear.

Software Versions and Operating Systems

Most technology users know that a particular software is not always used in the exact same way by all users. This is true for *Movie Maker* and *iMovie* as well. Newer versions of these programs are released to reflect new updates and additional features. Likewise, they operate in different ways depending on whether it performs on either a Windows or Macintosh operating system.

In this book, every effort has been made to create lessons and student steps that can be completed regardless of your software version or your operating system. If a lesson's procedure or student steps do not appear to work on your computer or with your version of *Movie Maker* or *iMovie*, refer to the program's Help menu for further assistance.

Teacher Resource CD

A Teacher Resource CD accompanies the *Learn & Use Movie Making in Your Classroom* book and includes supplementary materials that may be useful in your teaching. Student samples from various lessons, storyboard and shot list templates for student use, step-by-step directions pages and student directions pages for Macintosh and *Vista* users, and a blank rubric are all included. See pages 211–215 for further information.

How to Use This Book *(cont.)*

Components of the Program

Introduction

- Concise overview of effective use of technology in the classroom
- Brief introduction to software and the 16 featured skills
- Description of how to best utilize this product in the classroom
- Correlation to standards

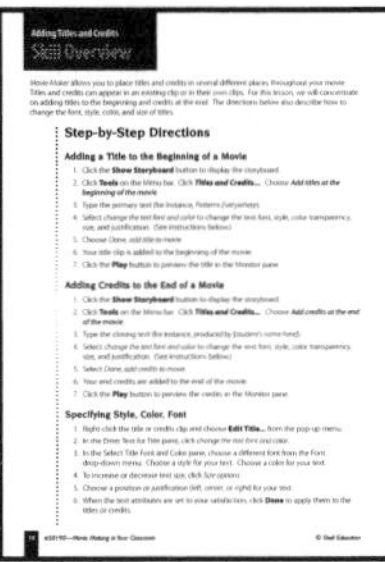

Step-by-Step Directions Pages

- Brief description of new skill(s) being introduced
- Detailed step-by-step instructions of new skill(s)
- Step-by-Step Directions pages for Macintosh and *Vista* users included on the Teacher Resource CD

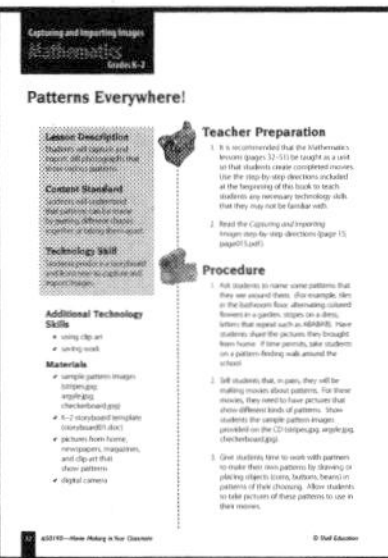

Procedure Sections

- Brief description of content-based lesson including content-standard and technology skills
- Materials list
- Suggestions for teacher preparation
- Detailed step-by-step sequential instructions for teaching the lesson
- Extension ideas for differentiation

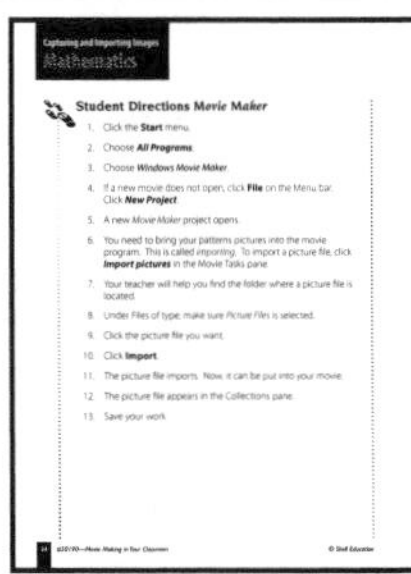

Student Directions

- List of steps for students to use while at the computers
- Help students complete the activity with little or no guidance
- Student Directions for Macintosh and *Vista* users included on the Teacher Resource CD

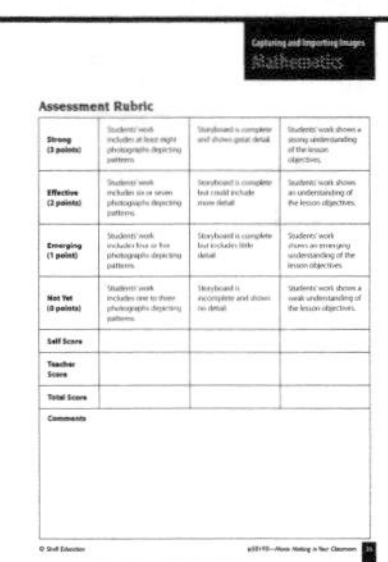

Rubrics

- Allow for standardized assessment of student work using specific criteria and a point grading scale
- Include space for both teacher and student to assess completed work
- Blank rubric included on the Teacher Resource CD

How to Use This Book *(cont.)*

Components of the Program *(cont.)*

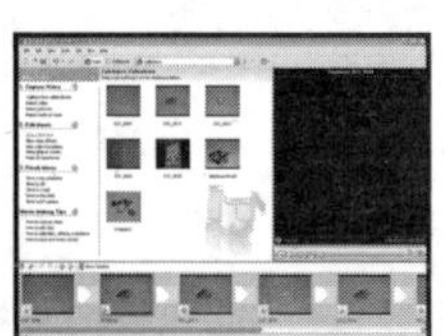

Student Samples

- Provides examples of what a project will look like when completed
- To be shown during the lesson to provide students further instruction and guidance

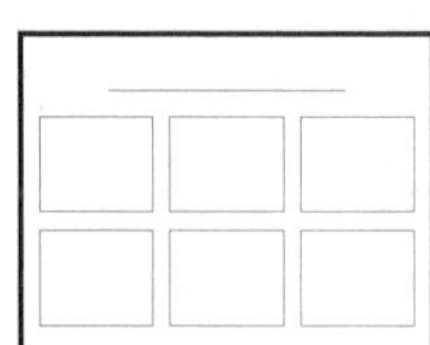

Storyboard and Shot List Templates

- Allows students to organize ideas and data before creating a movie

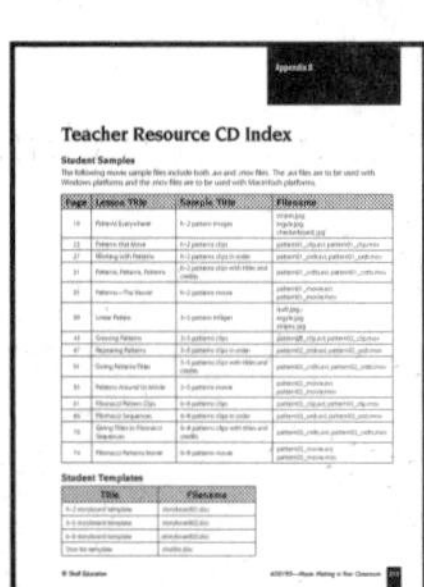

Appendices

- Works Cited and Other References
- Teacher Resource CD Index

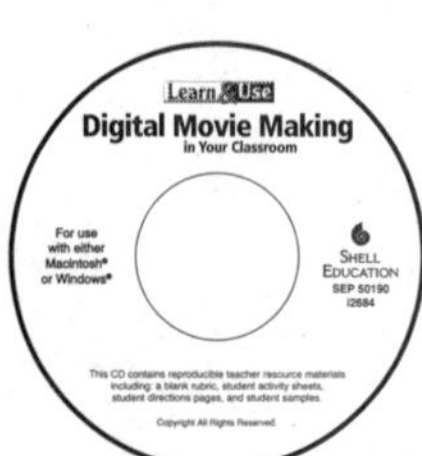

Teacher Resource CD

- Student samples
- Storyboard and shot list templates
- Student Directions pages
- Student Directions for Macintosh and *Vista* users
- Step-by-Step Directions pages
- Step-by-Step Directions pages for Macintosh and *Vista* users
- Blank rubric
- Learn & Use Series Description

Correlation to Standards

The No Child Left Behind (NCLB) legislation mandates that all states adopt academic standards that identify the skills students will learn in kindergarten through grade 12. While many states had already adopted academic standards prior to NCLB, the legislation set requirements to ensure the standards were detailed and comprehensive.

Standards are designed to focus instruction and guide adoption of curricula. Standards are statements that describe the criteria necessary for students to meet specific academic goals. They define the knowledge, skills, and content students should acquire at each level. Standards are also used to develop standardized tests to evaluate students' academic progress.

In many states today, teachers are required to demonstrate how their lessons meet state standards. State standards are used in the development of Shell Education products, so educators can be assured that this product meets strict academic requirements.

How to Find Your State Correlations

Shell Education is committed to producing educational materials that are research and standards based. In this effort, all products are correlated to the academic standards of the 50 states, the District of Columbia, and the Department of Defense Dependent Schools. A correlation report customized for your state can be printed directly from the Shell Education website: **http://www.shelleducation.com**. If you require assistance in printing correlation reports, please contact Customer Service at 1-800-877-3450.

McREL Compendium

Shell Education uses the Mid-continent Research for Education and Learning (McREL) Compendium to create standards correlations. Each year, McREL analyzes state standards and revises the compendium. By following this procedure, they are able to produce a general compilation of national standards. Each lesson in this book is based on one or more of the McREL content standards. The chart on the next two pages lists the McREL standards that correlate to each lesson used in the book.

Correlation to Standards *(cont.)*

Lesson Title	Technology Skill	Content Objective
Patterns Everywhere!	Students produce storyboards and learn how to capture and import images.	**Mathematics K–2:** Students will understand that patterns can be made by putting different shapes together or taking them apart.
Patterns That Move	Students view and rename clips and add clips to their movies.	
Working with Patterns	Students look at clips and arrange, add, or delete them.	
Patterns, Patterns, Patterns	Students add titles to the beginnings of their movies and insert credits at the ends of their movies. Students change the colors, fonts, styles, and sizes of their titles.	
Patterns—The Movie!	Students pick styles and transitions for their movies.	
States and Their Symbols	Students add titles before and after clips.	**Social Studies K–2:** Students will understand how symbols, slogans, and mottoes represent the states.
My State in Timeline	Students work with audio tracks.	
My State's Music	Students work with music tracks and add them to their movies.	
My State Clips	Students rearrange and delete clips from their movies.	
My State's Movie Style	Students use different styles or transitions to complete their movies.	
Saving the Planet One Step at a Time	Students use video effects in their movies.	**Science K–2:** Students will know that living things are found almost everywhere in the world and that distinct environments support the lives of different types of plants and animals.
Let's Save the Planet	Students record narration in their movies.	
Let's Save the Planet—The Mix	Students adjust the audio balance between the audio and the audio music tracks.	
Saving the Planet—The Movie	Students finalize their movies by choosing styles and transitions.	
Let's Share Our Work	Students share and save their work on recordable CDs and send them as email attachments.	
Linear Patterns	Students produce a shot list and storyboard and learn how to capture and import.	**Mathematics 3–5:** Students will recognize a wide variety of patterns and the rules that explain them.
Growing Patterns	Students view clips, rename clips, and add clips to their movies.	
Repeating Patterns	Students look at clips, arrange clips, and add or delete clips.	
Giving Patterns Titles	Students add titles to the beginnings of their movies and credits to the ends of their movies. Students change the colors, fonts, styles, and sizes of their titles.	
Patterns Around Us Movie	Students pick styles and transitions for their movies.	
My Country	Students add titles before and after clips.	**Social Studies 3–5:** Students will understand how various holidays reflect the shared values, principles, and beliefs of people.
My Country in Timeline	Students work with audio tracks recorded with a video camera.	
My Country's Music	Students work with music tracks and add them to their movies.	
My Country in Sequence	Students rearrange clips and delete clips from their movies.	
My Country Movie	Students use different styles or transitions to complete their movies.	

Correlation to Standards *(cont.)*

Lesson Title	Technology Skill	Content Objective
Our Environment—The Good, the Bad, and the Ugly	Students learn various techniques such as camera position and sound quality.	**Science 3–5:** Students will know that all organisms (including humans) cause changes in their environments, and these changes can be beneficial or detrimental.
Our Environment—The Commercial	Students use video effects in movies.	
The Voice of Our Environment	Students record narration for movies.	
Our Environment—Mixing Elements	Students adjust the audio balance between the audio and the audio music tracks.	
Our Environment—The Finished Commercial	Students save and share their commercials on recordable CDs and as email attachments.	
Fibonacci Patterns	Students produce a shot list and a storyboard.	**Mathematics 6–8:** Students will generalize from a pattern of observations made in particular cases, make conjectures, and provide supporting arguments for these conjectures.
Fibonacci Pattern Clips	Students capture and import images, view and rename clips, and add clips to their movies.	
Fibonacci Sequences	Students look at clips, arrange clips, and add or delete clips.	
Giving Titles to Fibonacci Sequences	Students add titles to the beginnings of their movies and credits to the ends of their movies. Students change the colors, fonts, styles, and sizes of their titles.	
Fibonacci Patterns Movie	Students pick styles and transitions for their movies.	
Historical Figures	Students add titles before and after clips.	**Social Studies 6–8:** Students will understand that specific individuals and the values those individuals held had impacts on history.
Historical Figures on a Timeline	Students work with audio tracks recorded with a video camera.	
Making Music Work	Students work with music tracks and add them to their movies.	
Sequencing the Movie	Students rearrange clips and delete clips from their movies.	
Historical Figures—The Video	Students use different styles or transitions to complete their movies.	
The Ecosystem—HELP!	Students learn various techniques such as camera position and sound quality.	**Science 6–8:** Students will know factors that affect the number and types of organisms an ecosystem can support (e.g., available resources; disease; competition from other organisms; predation).
The Ecosystem in 30 Seconds	Students use video effects in movies.	
The Ecosystem Speaks	Students record narration for movies.	
Sounds of the Ecosystem	Students adjust the audio balance between the audio and the audio music tracks.	
The Ecosystem—The Final Spot	Students save and share their commercials on recordable CDs and as email attachments.	

Skill Overview

Students will need to understand how to save their work because several class periods may be needed to complete their projects. The directions below describe how to start and save projects.

Step-by-Step Directions

Starting a New Project

1. Start *Movie Maker*.
2. If a new movie does not open, click **File** on the Menu bar.
3. Select ***New Project***.
4. A new *Movie Maker* project opens.

How to Save Your Project

1. Click **File** on the Menu bar.
2. Select ***Save Project***.
3. In the filename box, type the filename, and then click **Save**.

Skill Overview

Images that the students will be using need to be organized appropriately and captured and imported to the proper folder. The directions below describe how to capture and import images.

Step-by-Step Directions

Importing an Existing Picture File

1. In the Movie Tasks pane, click ***Import Pictures***.
2. Go to the folder where your picture file is located.
3. Under Files of type, make sure *Picture Files* is selected.
4. Click the desired picture file.
5. Click **Import**.
6. The picture file imports and appears in the Collections pane.

Capturing and Importing Video from a Camera

1. Turn on the camera and connect it to the computer with a FireWire. A FireWire is the connection between your digital camera and the computer.
2. Set the camera to VTR mode (some cameras call this Play or VCR).
3. In the Movie Tasks pane, click **Capture from video device**.
4. Enter the filename for your captured video file.
5. Choose a place to save your video file. Click **Next**.
6. Select the Video Setting (digital device format). Click **Next**.
7. Select the Capture Method to capture parts of the tape manually. Click **Next**.
8. Use the DV camera controls to locate the beginning of the video you want to capture.
9. Select ***Start Capture*** to begin capturing video.
10. Select ***Stop Capture*** to stop capturing video.
11. Click **Finish** to close the Video Capture Wizard.
12. Your captured clip is imported into the collection in the Contents pane.

Skill Overview

Images that the students will be working with need to be neat and organized in the Collections pane where they can be viewed and renamed. The Collections pane should be thought of as the library where all the images that have been imported are stored. The directions below describe how to use the Collections pane.

Step-by-Step Directions

Watching a Clip

1. Click the **Collections** button to bring up the Collections pane.
2. Choose the collection that contains the clip you want to watch.
3. In the Contents pane, click the clip you want to watch.
4. The clip appears in the Monitor pane.
5. Click the **Play** button to watch the clip. You can use the other Playback Controls to pause, stop, move forward or backward one frame at a time, fast forward, or rewind the clip.

Renaming a Clip

1. Right-click the clip you want to rename.
2. Choose **Rename** from the pop-up menu.
3. Type a new name for your clip.

Adding a Clip to Your Movie While in Storyboard View

1. Locate the clip you want to add to your movie.
2. Click, hold, and drag the clip down to the Timeline. As you move the clip over the Timeline, you will notice a vertical colored bar where it will be inserted if you let go of the mouse.
3. When the vertical colored bar is visible where you want your clip inserted, release the mouse. The clip is added to your movie.

Storyboard View shows the order of clips in your movie. It does not indicate how long each clip will be. Storyboard View is the easiest place to manage the sequence of clips. The directions below describe how to use Storyboard View. (Note: Clip Viewer is the *iMovie* equivalent.)

Step-by-Step Directions

General Information

1. You can scroll through the storyboard using the slider or scroll arrows.
2. You can use the playback controls to play, pause, and rewind the movie.

Arranging Clips on the Storyboard

1. Locate the clip you want to move.
2. Click, hold, and drag the desired clip along the storyboard. As you move the clip along the storyboard, you will notice a vertical colored bar where the clip will be relocated if you release the mouse.
3. When the vertical colored bar is visible where you want your clip moved, release the mouse, and the clip is moved to that position.

Adding a Clip to Storyboard View

1. Locate the clip you want to add into your movie. These clips should be in your Collections pane.
2. Click, hold, and drag the clip down to the storyboard. As you move the clip over the storyboard, you will notice a vertical colored bar where the clip will be inserted if you release the mouse.
3. When the vertical colored bar is visible where you want your clip inserted, release the mouse, and the clip is added to your movie.

Deleting a Clip from the Storyboard

1. Locate the clip you want to delete.
2. Right-click the clip.
3. Choose **Delete** from the pop-up menu.
4. The clip is deleted from your movie.

Importing an Existing Audio File

1. In the Task pane, click **Import Audio or Music**.
2. Go to the folder where your audio file is located.
3. Under Files of type, make sure *Audio and Music Files* is selected.
4. Click the desired audio file.
5. Click **Import**. The audio file imports.
6. The audio file appears in the Contents pane.

Skill Overview

Movie Maker allows you to place titles and credits in several different places throughout your movie. Titles and credits can appear in an existing clip or in their own clips. For this lesson, we will concentrate on adding titles to the beginning and credits at the end. The directions below also describe how to change the font, style, color, and size of titles.

Step-by-Step Directions

Adding a Title to the Beginning of a Movie

1. Click the **Show Storyboard** button to display the storyboard.
2. Click **Tools** on the Menu bar. Click ***Titles and Credits...***. Choose *Add titles at the beginning of the movie*.
3. Type the primary text (for instance, *Patterns Everywhere*).
4. Select *change the text font and color* to change the text font, style, color transparency, size, and justification. (See instructions below.)
5. Choose *Done, add title to movie*.
6. Your title clip is added to the beginning of the movie.
7. Click the **Play** button to preview the title in the Monitor pane.

Adding Credits to the End of a Movie

1. Click the **Show Storyboard** button to display the storyboard.
2. Click **Tools** on the Menu bar. Click ***Titles and Credits...***. Choose *Add credits at the end of the movie*.
3. Type the closing text (for instance, *produced by [student's name here]*).
4. Select *change the text font and color* to change the text font, style, color transparency, size, and justification. (See instructions below.)
5. Select *Done, add credits to movie*.
6. Your end credits are added to the end of the movie.
7. Click the **Play** button to preview the credits in the Monitor pane.

Specifying Style, Color, Font

1. Right-click the title or credits clip and choose **Edit Title...** from the pop-up menu.
2. In the Enter Text for Title pane, click *change the text font and color*.
3. In the Select Title Font and Color pane, choose a different font from the Font drop-down menu. Choose a style for your text. Choose a color for your text.
4. To increase or decrease text size, click *Size options*.
5. Choose a position or justification (*left*, *center*, or *right*) for your text.
6. When the text attributes are set to your satisfaction, click **Done** to apply them to the titles or credits.

AutoMovie is a shortcut to producing your movie. When making a movie such as the one in this series of lessons, using a predefined AutoMovie style would work best. An AutoMovie style determines how your titles and transitions look and behave.

To make an AutoMovie, you must first identify the clips you want to include in your movie. The clips and the titles you generated should already be in Storyboard View. Then, you choose an AutoMovie style. Finally, you finalize the movie with the click of the mouse. The directions below describe how to use AutoMovie.

Step-by-Step Directions

Selecting an AutoMovie Style

1. Click **Tools** on the Menu bar.
2. Select ***AutoMovie...***.
3. The AutoMovie wizard appears.
4. In the Select an AutoMovie Editing Style box, click on ***Highlights Movie*** style. The Highlights Movie creates a movie with cuts and fades between the clips, a title at the beginning, and credits at the end. A *cut* is a change from one shot to the other with no transition. A *fade* is a transition where the video or still image darkens to black, and then comes back up.
5. Click *Done, edit movie.*
6. All your transitions and titles are added to the storyboard.

Reviewing Your AutoMovie

1. Make sure the Playhead is at the beginning of the movie.
2. Click the Monitor pane's **Play** button to play the AutoMovie.

Skill Overview

Adding a title before a clip is a good way to introduce a new scene. Adding it after a clip is a good way to review a scene or to introduce the next scene. Both of these methods add a separate video clip to the video track before or after the selected clip.

Step-by-Step Directions

Adding Titles

1. Click the **Show Storyboard** button to display the Storyboard.
2. Click to select the clip that your title will precede or come after.
3. Click **Tools** on the Menu bar.
4. Click ***Titles and Credits...***.
5. Click *Add title before the selected clip on the storyboard* or *Add title after the selected clip on the storyboard*.
6. Type the main text you would like to include as the title. This is called the primary text.
7. Type any secondary (or smaller) text you want to include.
8. Select *Change the text font and color* to change the text, font, style floor, transparency, size, and justification.
9. Choose *Change the title animation* to specify how your title will animate in the movie. The animation determines how the title moves onto and off of the screen during playback.
10. Choose *Done, add title to movie.*
11. Your title clip is added before or after the clip as specified in Step 2.
12. Click the **Play** button to preview the title in the Monitor pane.
13. Save your movie.

Skill Overview

To add an audio file to your movie, you must first import it into a collection and then drag it to the Audio or Music track. You will find the Collection pane under **File** on the Menu bar.

Step-by-Step Directions

Importing an Audio File

1. In the Collections pane, click to select the collection where you want the audio file stored.
2. Click **File** on the Menu bar.
3. Click ***Import into Collections***.
4. Choose the folder that contains the desired audio file.
5. Click to select the audio file.
6. Click **Import**.
7. The audio file is added to the collection specified in Step 1.
8. Drag the audio clip to the desired location in the Audio or Music track in the Timeline.
9. The audio clip is added to your movie.

Skill Overview

Timeline View or Timeline Viewer gives you more information than Storyboard View or Clip Viewer. There are some tasks that you can only accomplish in Timeline View(er). For example, you can only work with audio tracks in Timeline View(er). Timeline View(er) is concerned more with time and less with sequence as opposed to the Storyboard View or Clip Viewer. It contains a great deal of information about the movie, and you can view all your tracks. Timeline View(er) also enables you to see how each clip fits within the time frame of the movie.

Step-by-Step Directions

Tracks

The Timeline displays the Video track, the Transitions track, the Audio track, the Audio or Music track, and the Title Overlay track. If you hold the mouse pointer over any clip in Timeline View, it will tell you the clip's duration.

1. **Video track**—This is the track that holds all the video clips in your movie. Any sound that is associated with the video will be on the Audio track. The Video track also holds *Titles and Credits* clips if they were added before or after a clip.
2. **Transition track**—This track holds any transitions you have added to your movie.
3. **Audio track**—The audio clips on this track are automatically placed here when you import videos that contain audio.
4. **Audio/Music track**—This track contains any other audio you have added to your movie, such as sound effects, songs, or recorded narration.
5. **Title Overlay track**—This track holds *Titles of Credits* clips if they were added on a clip.

Audio

You can adjust the audio balance between the Audio and Audio or Music tracks, which affects the audio level throughout the entire movie. You can also change the volume of the individual clips in the Audio track (the audio that was captured as part of a video clip). You can use the **Set Audio Levels** button to adjust the audio tracks' volume.

1. Click the **Set Audio Levels** button in the Timeline. You can also click **Tools** on the Menu bar and then click ***Audio Levels***.
2. Drag the slider to adjust the audio balance. Dragging it to the right will increase the audio or music volume level while decreasing the audio from the video volume level. Dragging it to the left will do the opposite.
3. When you are done, click the **X** in the upper right-hand corner of the box to close the Audio Levels dialog box.

Playback Controls

You can use these controls to play, pause, and rewind your movie.

Skill Overview

To add music (audio files) to your movie, you must first import them into a collection and then drag them to the Audio or Music track. You will find the Collection pane under **File** on the Menu bar.

Step-by-Step Directions

Adding audio from a CD

1. Place the audio CD into your CD or DVD drive.
2. Click the **Audio** button to bring up the audio pane.
3. The CD title will show in the pull-down menu.
4. Locate the song you want to import into your movie.
5. Drag the song from the Audio pane to the desired position on the Timeline.
6. The CD audio is inserted in the Timeline.

Rearranging Clip Sequences and Deleting Clips

Skill Overview

You can rearrange the clip sequence in Storyboard View (Clip Viewer) or Timeline View. The directions below show Timeline View, but it is done the same way while in Storyboard View (Clip Viewer).

Step-by-Step Directions

Rearranging Clip Sequence

1. Locate the clip you want to rearrange.
2. Click, hold, and drag the desired clip along the Timeline. As you move the clip along the Timeline, you will notice a vertical colored bar where it will be rearranged if you let go of the mouse.
3. When the vertical colored bar is visible where you want your clip to be rearranged, release the mouse, and the clip is rearranged to that position.

Deleting a Clip from Your Movie

1. Locate the clip you want to delete.
2. Right-click the clip.
3. Choose **Delete** from the pop-up menu.
4. The clip is deleted from your movie.

Skill Overview

Adding transitions and style to your movie is an important part of completing a project. In AutoMovie, there are different styles from which you can choose. Each one gives a different look and feel to your finished movie.

Step-by-Step Directions

Selecting an AutoMovie Style

1. Click **Tools** on the Menu bar.
2. Select ***AutoMovie...***.
3. The AutoMovie wizard appears.
4. Select an AutoMovie editing style from the box.
5. Click *Done, edit movie.*

AutoMovie Styles

The following AutoMovie editing styles should be considered for the movie:

1. **Highlights Movie**—This movie style has cuts and fades between clips, a title at the beginning, and credits at the end.
2. **Music Video**—This style adds quick edits for a fast pace and long edits for slower clips based on the music track's beat.
3. **Sports Highlights**—This style adds excitement to the movie with exploding titles and credits that wrap around the movie. It includes fast pans and zooms between clips.

Skill Overview

There are details to consider when filming or videotaping a movie. These details include various camera angles, camera movements, and camera shots. There are also a few key suggestions that will help make your audio clear.

Important Vocabulary

Camera Angles

- **Flat shot**—The subject and the camera are at the same angle.
- **High angle**—The camera is at a point higher than the subject.
- **Low angle**—The camera is at a point lower than the subject.
- **Overhead**—The camera is looking down on a subject.

Camera Movements

- **Pan**—A pan is the horizontal pivoting of the camera to the right or left. Pans are best executed slowly and with purpose.
- **Tilt**—A tilt is the vertical pivoting of the camera up or down. Like a pan, a tilt is best executed slowly and with purpose.
- **Zoom**—A zoom is a camera lens movement (the camera stays stationary) that reduces or magnifies the subject and the field of view.
- **Dolly**—A dolly is a horizontal movement of the camera towards or away from the action. A dolly has the effect of bringing your viewer closer or farther away from the subject.

Camera Shots

- **Wide or Long Shot**—The wide or long shot frames a wide field of the subject and its surroundings.
- **Medium**—A medium shot includes more of the subject than a long shot and still includes some background. A medium shot shows more detail than a long shot.
- **Close-Up**—A close-up shot is for showing detail.
- **Extreme Close-up**—An extreme close-up shot frames only a portion of your subject.

Shooting Video to Edit

1. Start the tape rolling several seconds before a shot starts, and keep it rolling when the action is over. It is easy to crop when editing.
2. Shoot more than one take if you can. Try to shoot both medium and close-up shots.
3. When you are starting at a new location, begin with a wide shot that identifies where you are.
4. Use different angles throughout your movie.

Audio Considerations

Most digital camcorders today have built-in microphones of sufficient quality. If possible, try to use headphones while recording. Wearing headphones will help you hear exactly what the camera hears.

Skill Overview

Video effects let you add special effects to your movie. There are more than 20 video effects to choose from. A video effect is applied for the entire duration that the specific video clip, picture, or title displays in your movie. You can add any of the video effects that appear in the Video Effects folder in the Collections pane. You can add video effects to single or multiple clips. Use video effects sparingly. Remember the focus of your project should be on the content of your movie and not on the special effects. However, when used appropriately, video effects can add to and support your content.

Step-by-Step Directions

Accessing Effects

1. You can access the video effects by clicking on the ***Video Effects*** folder in the Collections pane.
2. There are 28 video effects available to use. You can see them all by scrolling in the Video Effects pane.
3. The blue star icon in the lower left corner of the clip indicates that a video effect has been applied to the clip.

Previewing Video Effects

1. Click **Collections**.
2. Click the ***Video Effects*** folder in the Collections pane.
3. Double-click the video effect you want to preview.
4. The video effect is previewed in the Monitor pane.

Adding a Video Effect to a Clip

1. Click **Collections**.
2. Click the ***Video Effects*** folder in the Collections pane.
3. Click, hold, and drag the desired effect to your chosen clip in the Storyboard or Timeline.
4. The effects icon on the clip turns from gray to blue, indicating that the effect has been added.

Deleting a Video Effect from a Clip

1. On the clip from which you want to delete the video effect (while in Storyboard View), right-click the Effect icon in the lower-left corner of the clip.
2. Click **Delete Effects**.
3. The star turns from blue to gray, indicating that the video effect has been deleted.

Skill Overview

Movie Maker has a built-in narration feature allowing you to record an Audio track that coincides with the Video track. When you have your narration, *Movie Maker* adds it to the Audio or Music track.

Step-by-Step Directions

1. In Timeline View, drag the Playhead to the location where you want to start the narration.
2. Click **Narrate Timeline**.
3. In the Narrate Timeline dialog box, adjust the Input level. As you speak, your voice should fall into the green area and rarely or never go into the red.
4. Click ***Start Narration*** and begin speaking. *Movie Maker* plays the video while you record, allowing you to time your narration to the movie.
5. Click ***Stop Narration***.
6. Enter a filename for your narration. *Movie Maker* automatically saves the narration into a folder called *Narration*, located in the *My Videos* folder with the rest of your clips.
7. Click **Save**.
8. Your narration appears in the Timeline, beginning at the location you specified in step 1.

You can adjust the audio balance between the Audio and Audio or Music tracks, which affects the audio level throughout the entire movie. You can also change the volume of individual clips in the Audio track (the audio that was captured as part of a video clip) and individual clips in the Audio or Music track (audio that was captured or imported independently of video clips).

Step-by-Step Directions

Changing a Clip's Volume

1. Right-click the audio clip that you want to adjust.
2. Choose **Volume** from the contextual menu.
3. Drag the slider to adjust the volume.
4. Select **OK**.
5. The volume is changed. The waveform of the clip visually represents the volume change.

Adjusting Audio Balance

1. Click the **Set Audio Levels** button in the Timeline.
2. Drag the slider to adjust the audio balance. Dragging it to the right will increase the Audio or Music volume level while decreasing the Audio from Video volume level. Dragging it to the left will do the opposite.
3. When you are done, click the **X** in the upper right-hand corner of the box to close the Audio Levels dialog box.

Muting Sound

You can mute the sound in any clip you wish. This is handy if you have a sound in the Audio or Music track and do not want the sound in the Audio track to play.

1. Right-click the audio clip for which you want to mute the volume.
2. Choose **Mute** from the contextual menu.
3. The sound is muted. The waveform of the clip visually represents the volume change.

Skill Overview

AutoMovie is a shortcut to producing your movie. When making a movie, using a predefined AutoMovie style would work best. An AutoMovie style determines how your titles and transitions look and behave. To make an AutoMovie, you must first identify the clips you want to include in your movie. These clips and the titles you generated should already be in Storyboard View. You then choose an AutoMovie style.

Step-by-Step Directions

Selecting an AutoMovie Style

1. Click **Tools** on the Menu bar.
2. Select ***AutoMovie***.
3. The AutoMovie wizard appears.
4. Select an AutoMovie editing style.
5. Click *Done, edit movie.*
6. All your transitions and titles are added to the Storyboard.

Reviewing Your AutoMovie

1. Make sure the Playhead is at the beginning of the movie.
2. Click the Monitor pane's **Play** button to play the AutoMovie.

There are several choices for saving a movie. This option will allow almost anyone to play back your movie on his or her computer as long as it has a CD drive. When you choose this option, *Movie Maker* saves the movie directly to a recordable CD.

Step-by-Step Directions

Saving the Final Movie to a CD

1. Click **Tasks**.
2. Under Finish Movie, click ***Save to CD***.
3. In the Save Movie wizard, type a filename for your saved movie.
4. Type a name for the CD.
5. Click *Next* at the bottom of the window.
6. Click *Next* again.
7. Depending on the length of your movie, it may take several minutes to save.
8. If you want to save the movie to another CD, click the *Save the movie to another recordable CD* box.
9. Click **Finish**.
10. Your movie is saved.

Saving the Final Movie As an Email Attachment

This option prepares your movie as an email attachment, automatically launching your email application and creating a new message with the movie attached. You also have the option of saving the movie to your hard drive.

1. Click **Tasks**.
2. Under Finish Movie, click ***Send in email***.
3. Depending on the length of your movie, it might take a few minutes to save.
4. If you want to save a copy of the movie on your computer, click *Save a copy of the movie on my computer*.
5. Select *Next* at the bottom of the window.
6. Your email application opens, and a new email is created with the movie attached.
7. Type in an email address.
8. Type a message.
9. Click **Send**.

Patterns Everywhere!

Lesson Description

Students will capture and import still photographs that show various patterns.

Content Standard

Students will understand that patterns can be made by putting different shapes together or taking them apart.

Technology Skill

Students produce a storyboard and learn how to capture and import images.

Additional Technology Skills

- using clip art
- saving work

Materials

- sample pattern images (stripes.jpg; argyle.jpg; checkerboard.jpg)
- K–2 storyboard template (storyboard01.doc)
- pictures from home, newspapers, magazines, and clip art that show patterns
- digital camera

Teacher Preparation

1. It is recommended that the Mathematics lessons (pages 32–51) be taught as a unit so that students create completed movies. Use the step-by-step directions included at the beginning of this book to teach students any necessary technology skills that they may not be familiar with.

2. Read the *Capturing and Importing Images* step-by-step directions (page 15; page015.pdf).

Procedure

1. Ask students to name some patterns that they see around them. (For example, tiles in the bathroom floor, alternating colored flowers in a garden, stripes on a dress, letters that repeat such as ABABAB). If time permits, take students on a pattern-finding walk around the school.

2. Tell students that, in pairs, they will be making movies about patterns. For these movies, they need to have pictures that show different kinds of patterns. Show students the sample pattern images provided on the CD (stripes.jpg, argyle.jpg, checkerboard.jpg).

3. Give students time to work with partners to make their own patterns by drawing or placing objects (coins, buttons, beans) in patterns of their choosing. Allow students to take pictures of these patterns to use in their movies.

Procedure *(cont.)*

4. Explain to students that before they can make movies, they must create storyboards. A storyboard should include a sketch for each pattern a student includes in the movie. There should be only one sketch per frame on a storyboard.

5. Distribute copies of the K–2 storyboard template (storyboard01.doc) to students. Give them time to work on their storyboards in pairs.

6. Then, students should research and gather the patterns in their storyboards using clip art, magazines, digital cameras, and the Internet. To check for understanding, walk around the room and ask each pair if its photographs show patterns. Ask what kinds of patterns each student sees.

7. Explain to students that in this lesson they are going to learn how to capture and import the photographs and videos they take. The images that they take need to be neatly organized, captured, and imported into the proper folder. So, make sure you help them save all the images they have found in one place. It is a good idea to have them name the folders with their own names or the name of the project, *Patterns*.

8. Work with students to capture and import their images. Since you need to help each pair, this step may take more than one lesson. Show students how and where to save their finished work.

9. Explain to students that this is the first step in the process of making their movies. They should continue looking for new patterns and challenge themselves to find ones that are even better than the ones they are working with now. The more material they have to work with, the more editing choices they will have. Remind them that it is better to have too many choices than not enough.

10. Review the rubric (page 35) with students so that they understand how their work will be assessed.

Extension Idea

Have students create at least two more storyboard frames that show patterns in their classroom or school. They should add these patterns and pictures to their movies.

Student Directions *Movie Maker*

1. Click the **Start** menu.
2. Choose ***All Programs***.
3. Choose *Windows Movie Maker*.
4. If a new movie does not open, click **File** on the Menu bar. Click ***New Project***.
5. A new *Movie Maker* project opens.
6. You need to bring your patterns pictures into the movie program. This is called *importing*. To import a picture file, click ***Import pictures*** in the Movie Tasks pane.
7. Your teacher will help you find the folder where a picture file is located.
8. Under Files of type; make sure *Picture Files* is selected.
9. Click the picture file you want.
10. Click **Import**.
11. The picture file imports. Now, it can be put into your movie.
12. The picture file appears in the Collections pane.
13. Save your work.

Assessment Rubric

Strong (3 points)	Students' work includes at least eight photographs depicting patterns.	Storyboard is complete and shows great detail.	Students' work shows a strong understanding of the lesson objectives.
Effective (2 points)	Students' work includes six or seven photographs depicting patterns.	Storyboard is complete but could include more detail.	Students' work shows an understanding of the lesson objectives.
Emerging (1 point)	Students' work includes four or five photographs depicting patterns.	Storyboard is complete but includes little detail.	Students' work shows an emerging understanding of the lesson objectives.
Not Yet (0 points)	Students' work includes one to three photographs depicting patterns.	Storyboard is incomplete and shows no detail.	Students' work shows a weak understanding of the lesson objectives.
Self Score			
Teacher Score			
Total Score			
Comments			

Patterns That Move

Lesson Description

Students will learn to work with clips they have already captured and imported that show various patterns.

Content Standard

Students will understand that patterns can be made by putting different shapes together or taking them apart.

Technology Skill

Students view and rename clips and add clips to their movies.

Additional Technology Skills

- capturing and importing images
- saving work
- filming a video

Materials

- K–2 patterns clips sample (pattern01_clip.avi; pattern01_clip.mov)
- video clips that show patterns
- video camera
- digital camera

Teacher Preparation

1. Use the step-by-step directions included at the beginning of this book to teach students any necessary technology skills that they may not be familiar with.
2. Read the *Working with Clips* step-by-step directions (page 16; page016.pdf).

Procedure

1. Remind students of the previous lesson about patterns (*Patterns Everywhere!*). Ask them if they have noticed any new or unusual patterns around them. Let them share. Explain to students that they will be learning how to work with clips they have already captured and imported.

2. Ask students if they have any new photographs they would like to add to their projects.

3a. Model for students how to open their saved work. Start *Movie Maker*. Click **File** on the Menu bar. Click ***Open Project***. Go to the folder where the project is saved. Click the project you want to open. Click **Open**. Show a particular student's saved project.

3b. If using a Macintosh, start *iMovie*. Click **File**; click ***Open Project***. Go to the folder where the project is saved, click the project you want to open, and click **Open**.

4. Give student pairs time to review their projects and to capture and import any new photographs. You may need to meet with each pair to help them.

Procedure *(cont.)*

5. Bring the class back together to review the new technology skill—working with clips. Show students the sample K–2 clips provided on the CD (pattern01_clip.avi; pattern01_clip.mov), and talk about them.

6. To show how students can make a clip about patterns, have students stand in a straight line. The first student will bend his or her knees. The next student will stand on his or her toes. The third student will bend his or her knees. This pattern will repeat over and over in that same order. Record this, or take a photograph and import it onto the computer.

7. Discuss other clips that could show patterns. Let students share or demonstrate their ideas. Record these ideas using a video camera or digital camera for the students to use in their movies.

8. Explain to students that they will need some pattern clips for their movies. Clips will be saved in the Collections pane. Collections are libraries that contain all the pictures that they have imported. They can use and reuse items from the collections for the movies they create. The Collections pane is found in the **File** menu. (If using a Macintosh, clips will be saved in the Clips pane.)

9a. Model for students how to view a clip. First, click **Collections**. Then, choose the collection that contains the clip you want to watch. In the Contents pane, click the clip you want to watch. The clip appears on the monitor pane, click the **Play** button and watch your clip.

9b. If using a Macintosh, click the **Clips** button to bring up the Clips pane. In the Clips pane, click the clip you want to watch. The clip appears in the Monitor window. Click the **Play** button to watch your clip. You can also drag the slider bar to move quickly through the clip.

10a. Model for students how to rename a clip. Right-click the clip you want to rename. Choose **Rename**. Type a new name for your clip.

10b. If using a Macintosh, double-click the clip you want to rename. Type a new name in the *Name* field. Click **Set**, and your clip is renamed.

11. Show students how and where to save their work.

12. Remind students that this is an ongoing project, so they should keep looking for patterns.

13. Review the rubric (page 39) with students so that they understand how their work will be assessed.

Extension Idea

Challenge students to videotape patterns in their homes and bring in the files to use in their movies.

Student Directions *Movie Maker*

1. Turn your camera on. Help your teacher connect it to the computer.
2. Set the camera to VTR mode. (Some cameras call this Play or VCR.)
3. Go to the Movie Tasks pane. Click **Capture from the video device**.
4. Type a filename for your file. Your teacher will tell you where to save your file. Click **Next**.
5. Select ***Digital device format***. This is the Video Setting. Click **Next**.
6. Select the Capture Method. You want to capture parts of the tape manually. Click **Next**.
7. Help your teacher use the camera controls to locate the part of the video you want to record.
8. Together, select ***Start Capture***. This will begin recording the video.
9. Click ***Stop Capture*** when you want to stop recording the video.
10. Click **Finish**. This will close the Video Capture wizard. Your video clip is saved. It is in the collection in the Contents pane.
11. Click the **Play** button to watch the clip.
12. Now, it is time to move the clip into your movie. Click on the clip. Hold the mouse button down. Drag the clip down to the Timeline.
13. When the colored bar is where you want your clip to be, let go of the mouse button. The clip is added to your movie.
14. Save your work.

Assessment Rubric

Strong (3 points)	Students included at least three new clips for their movies.	All the clips the students chose depict patterns.	Imported video clips contain focused content that supports the project.	Students' work shows a strong understanding of the lesson objectives.
Effective (2 points)	Students included at least two new clips for their movies.	Most of the clips the students chose depict patterns.	Imported video clips support the project.	Students' work shows an understanding of the lesson objectives.
Emerging (1 point)	Students included at least one new clip for their movies.	Few of the clips the students chose depict patterns.	Imported video clips support the project. Some could be more focused.	Students' work shows an emerging understanding of the lesson objectives.
Not Yet (0 points)	Students did not include any new clips.	None of the clips the students chose depict patterns.	Imported video clips did not support the project.	Students' work shows a weak understanding of the lesson objectives.
Self Score				
Teacher Score				
Total Score				
Comments				

Working with Patterns

Lesson Description

Students will learn to take the clips that they have already captured and stored and add them to Storyboard View or Clip Viewer.

Content Standard

Students will understand that patterns can be made by putting different shapes together or taking them apart.

Technology Skills

Students look at clips and arrange, add, or delete them.

Additional Technology Skill

- saving work

Materials

- K–2 patterns clips in order sample (pattern01_ordr.avi; pattern01_ordr.mov)

Teacher Preparation

1. Use the step-by-step directions included at the beginning of this book to teach students any necessary technology skills that they may not be familiar with.

2. Read the *Working in Storyboard View or Clip Viewer* step-by-step directions (page 17; page017.pdf).

Procedure

1. Remind students of the previous lessons about patterns (*Patterns Everywhere!* and *Patterns That Move*). Today is a continuation of those lessons.

2. Let student pairs add any new clips or images to their movies.

3a. Model for students how to open their saved work. Start *Movie Maker*. Click **File** on the Menu bar. Click ***Open Project***. Go to the folder where your project is saved. Click the project you want to open. Click **Open**. Show a student's saved project.

3b. If using a Macintosh, start *iMovie*. Click **File**; click ***Open Project***. Go to the folder where your project is saved, click the project you want to open, and click **Open**.

4. Ask a student to talk about his or her favorite movie. When the student is finished, ask the other students if the movie would have made sense if the end had come at the beginning and the middle was at the end? Most students will probably say that the movie would not make sense in that order.

Procedure *(cont.)*

5. Remind students that events in movies (and all other stories) are in a certain order to make sense. Their movies need to be in an order to make sense, too. Show students the sample provided on the CD (pattern01_ordr.avi; pattern01_ordr.mov). Tell students that they will be organizing and arranging the clips that they have already captured and imported with Storyboard View or Clip Viewer.

6. Explain that Storyboard View or Clip Viewer is the next step in the process of making their movies. Storyboard View or Clip Viewer shows the sequence of the clips in their movies.

7. Explain to students that with this technology, they will be able to put their clips in order, delete any clips that are not working for them, add any new clips they have, and arrange them in order for their movies. Give them time to practice moving clips, adding clips, and arranging them.

8. Remind students to continue to look for patterns. Challenge them to improve upon the photographs of patterns that they already have for the next lesson.

9. Remind students to save their work.

10. Review the rubric (page 43) with students so that they understand how their work will be assessed.

Extension Idea

Have students arrange their clips in four different sequences to see which one works best. They can do this by adding, deleting, or rearranging their clips.

Student Directions *Movie Maker*

1. Put your movie clips in the right order. You need to make sure your movie tells a story.
2. Click on a clip you want to move. Hold your mouse button down. Drag the clip along the storyboard.
3. When the colored bar is visible where you want to put the clip, let go of the mouse button.
4. Find a new clip you want to add into your movie. These clips should be in your Collections pane.
5. Click on the clip. Hold your mouse button down. Drag the clip down to the storyboard.
6. When the colored bar is where you want to put your clip, let go of the mouse button. The clip is added to your movie.
7. To delete a clip, find the clip you want to delete. Right-click the clip.
8. Choose **Delete** from the pop-up menu. The clip is deleted from your movie.
9. Save your work.

Assessment Rubric

Strong (3 points)	Students were creative in arranging the sequence in Storyboard View or Clip Viewer by experimenting with adding, deleting, and rearranging their photographs.	Students' work shows a strong understanding of the lesson objectives.
Effective (2 points)	Students experimented in Storyboard View or Clip Viewer by adding and rearranging their photographs.	Students' work shows an understanding of the lesson objectives.
Emerging (1 point)	Students experimented with Storyboard View or Clip Viewer by rearranging their photographs.	Students' work shows an emerging understanding of the lesson objectives.
Not Yet (0 points)	Students did not experiment with Storyboard View or Clip Viewer.	Students' work shows a weak understanding of the lesson objectives.
Self Score		
Teacher Score		
Total Score		
Comments		

Patterns, Patterns, Patterns

Lesson Description

Students will add titles and credits to their movies as well as change the colors, fonts, styles, and sizes of their titles.

Content Standard

Students will understand that patterns can be made by putting different shapes together or taking them apart.

Technology Skills

Students add titles to the beginnings of their movies and insert credits at the ends of their movies. Students change the colors, fonts, styles, and sizes of their titles.

Additional Technology Skills

- saving work
- using Storyboard View or Clip Viewer

Materials

- K–2 patterns movie sample with titles and credits (pattern01_crdts.avi; pattern01_crdts.mov)

Teacher Preparation

1. Use the step-by-step directions included at the beginning of this book to teach students any necessary technology skills that they may not be familiar with.

2. Read the *Adding Titles and Credits* step-by-step directions (page 18; page018.pdf).

Procedure

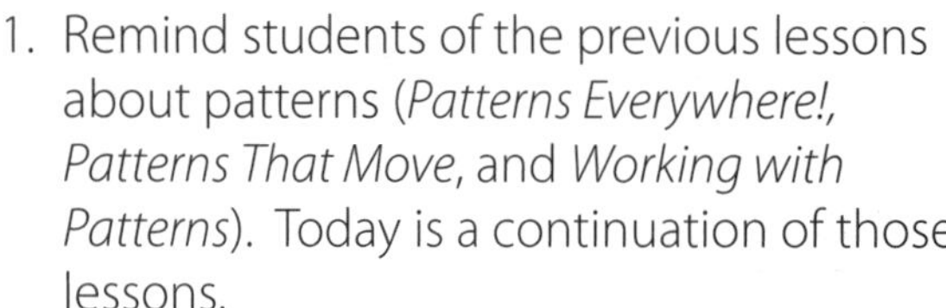

1. Remind students of the previous lessons about patterns (*Patterns Everywhere!*, *Patterns That Move*, and *Working with Patterns*). Today is a continuation of those lessons.

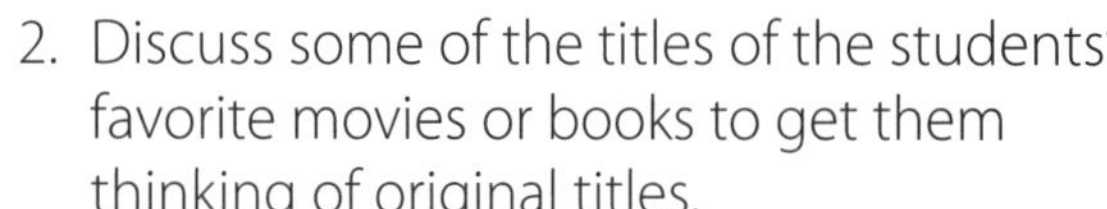

2. Discuss some of the titles of the students' favorite movies or books to get them thinking of original titles.

3. Write the word *fractions* on the board. Brainstorm with the class what titles they think would work for a movie about fractions. You could suggest the title, *Going to Pieces*. Remind them that titles are often funny or interesting.

4. Once they come up with titles, explain that they will be doing the same thing for their movies about patterns.

Procedure *(cont.)*

5. Tell students that any text that they add to a movie (anywhere in the movie) could be a title. Titles can be added at the beginning, at the end, over an existing clip, and before or after a clip. For this lesson, they will learn how to add titles at the beginnings and ends of their movies. The titles at the ends of movies are called *credits*. The credits tell about the people involved in making the movie. Show students the sample clips on the CD (pattern01_crdts.avi; pattern01_crdts.mov).

6. Have students work with partners to come up with creative, fun, and interesting titles for their movies.

7. Explain to students that they will have opportunities to change the color, font, style, and size of their titles.

8. Review the technology skill to be used—adding titles. Adding a title at the beginning is a good way to introduce the movie title. Credits at the end are titles that conclude the movie. Changing the color, font, style, and size is a good way to be creative with titles.

9. Give students time to open their projects, review their projects to date, and add titles and credits.

10. Remind students to save their finished work.

11. Review the rubric (page 47) with students so they understand how their work will be assessed.

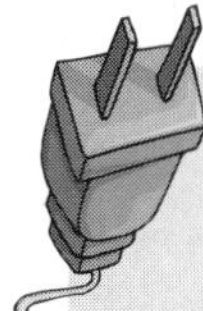

Extension Idea

Have the students experiment with adding titles before a clip or photo. Adding a title before a clip is a good way to introduce a new scene.

Student Directions *Movie Maker*

1. It is time to add a title to the beginning of your movie. Click the **Show Storyboard** button.
2. Click **Tools** on the Menu bar. Click ***Titles and Credits...***. Choose *Add titles at the beginning of the movie*.
3. Type the name of your movie.
4. Click *Done, add title to movie*. Your title clip is added to the beginning of the movie.
5. Click the **Play** button. That way, you can preview the title in the Monitor pane.
6. Now, add credits to your movie. Click **Tools** on the Menu bar. Click ***Titles and Credits...***. Choose *Add credits at the end of the movie*.
7. Type the credits. This should be your name and your partner's name.
8. Click *Done, add title to movie*. Your ending credits are added to the end of the movie.
9. Click the **Play** button to preview the title in the Monitor pane.
10. To change the style, color, or font, right-click the title or credits clip and choose **Edit Title...** from the pop-up menu.
11. In the Enter Text for Title pane, click *Change the text font and color*.
12. In the Select Title Font and Color pane, choose a different font from the Font drop-down menu.
13. Choose a style and color for your text. To increase or decrease text size, click *Size options*.
14. Choose a position or justification for your text. You can align the text on the left, in the center, or on the right.
15. When the text attributes are set to your satisfaction, click **Done** to apply them to the titles or credits.
16. Save your work.

Assessment Rubric

Strong (3 points)	Movie includes an opening title and closing credits that accurately describe the movie.	Creative use of fonts, styles, colors, and sizes create visually appealing opening title and closing credits.	Students' work shows a strong understanding of the lesson objectives.
Effective (2 points)	Movie includes an opening title and closing credits.	Students were able to use font, style, color, and size applications in either the title or credits but not both.	Students' work shows an understanding of the lesson objectives.
Emerging (1 point)	Movie includes either an opening title or closing credits but not both.	Students used one of the font, style, color, or size applications.	Students' work shows an emerging understanding of the lesson objectives.
Not Yet (0 points)	Movie does not include title or credits.	Students did not use font, style, color, or size applications.	Students' work shows a weak understanding of the lesson objectives.
Self Score			
Teacher Score			
Total Score			

Comments

Patterns—The Movie!

Lesson Description

Students will use AutoMovie or Magic iMovie to complete their movies.

Content Standard

Students will understand that patterns can be made by putting different shapes together or taking them apart.

Technology Skills

Students pick styles and transitions for their movies.

Additional Technology Skills

- using Storyboard View or Clip Viewer
- saving work

Materials

- K–2 patterns movie sample (pattern01_movie.avi; pattern01_movie.mov)

Teacher Preparation

1. Use the step-by-step directions included at the beginning of this book to teach students any necessary technology skills that they may not be familiar with.
2. Read the *Using AutoMovie or Magic iMovie* step-by-step directions (page 19; page019.pdf).
3. Let the students know that they will be finishing their movies. Explain to them that this will be their last opportunity to add any new materials to these projects.

Procedure

1. Remind students of the previous lessons about patterns (*Patterns Everywhere!*, *Patterns That Move*, *Working with Patterns*, and *Patterns, Patterns, Patterns*). Today is a continuation of those lessons.
2. Explain to students that they will be finishing their movies today with the technology called AutoMovie or Magic iMovie.
3. Review how to use AutoMovie or Magic iMovie. Explain that these are shortcuts for producing movies. AutoMovie or Magic iMovie will build and edit the movies based on the clips and titles stored in Storyboard View or Clip Viewer.
4. Show students the sample movie provided on the CD (pattern01_movie.avi, pattern01_movie.mov).

Procedure *(cont.)*

5a. Model for students how to open their saved work. Start *Movie Maker*. Click **File** on the Menu bar. Click ***Open Project***. Go to folder where your project is saved. Click the project you want to open. Click **Open**. Show a student's saved project.

5b. If using a Macintosh, start *iMovie*. Click **File**; click ***Open Project***. Go to the folder where your project is saved, click the project you want to open, and click **Open**.

6. Give student pairs time to review their saved work and to capture and import any new photographs.
7. Review how to add titles and credits and how to change the color, font, style, and size of the titles.
8. Have the students review their movies two or three times to see if there are any changes that need to be made. If so, have them make the changes.
9. Remind the students to save their work.
10. When the students have completed their movies, allow them to play their movies for the class.
11. Review the rubric (page 51) with students so that they understand how their work will be assessed.

Extension Idea

Have students experiment with different AutoMovie styles. For this project, the other styles to experiment with are Flip and Slide (transitions include flip, slide, reveal, and page curl) and Sports Highlights (adds excitement with exploding titles, end credits that wrap around your video including fast pans, and zoom between clips). In *iMovie*, they can experiment with Random Choice.

Student Directions *Movie Maker*

1. Click **Tools** on the Menu bar.
2. Click ***AutoMovie...***.
3. The AutoMovie wizard appears.
4. Click the ***Highlights Movie*** style.
5. Click *Done, edit movie*.
6. Your movie is almost ready.
7 Make sure the Playhead is at the beginning of your movie.
8. Click the Monitor pane's **Play** button to play the AutoMovie.
9. Save your work.

Assessment Rubric

Strong (3 points)	Students included at least three video clips in the movie.	Movie is visually appealing, and the titles improve the presentation.	Students completed the work independently.	Students' work shows a strong understanding of the lesson objectives.
Effective (2 points)	Students included at least two video clips in the movie.	Movie is visually appealing.	Students completed the work with some support.	Students' work shows an understanding of the lesson objectives.
Emerging (1 point)	Students included one video clip in the movie.	Movie is somewhat visually appealing.	Students completed the work with a lot of support.	Students' work shows an emerging understanding of the lesson objectives.
Not Yet (0 points)	Students did not include any video clips in the movie.	Movie is visually unappealing, and no titles were used.	Students did not complete the work.	Students' work shows a weak understanding of the lesson objectives.
Self Score				
Teacher Score				
Total Score				

Comments

States and Their Symbols

Lesson Description

Students will learn how to add titles before and after clips that they have already captured and imported in Storyboard View or Clip Viewer.

Content Standard

Students will understand how symbols, slogans, and mottoes represent the states.

Technology Skill

Students add titles before and after clips.

Additional Technology Skills

- saving work
- capturing and importing video
- using Storyboard View or Clip Viewer

Materials

- digital camera
- video camera
- storyboard template (storyboard01.doc)
- pictures from home, newspapers, magazines, clip art, or the Internet of state symbols, slogans, or mottoes
- video clips from home of state symbols, slogans, or mottoes

Teacher Preparation

1. It is recommended that the Social Studies lessons (pages 52–71) be taught as a unit so that students create completed movies. Use the step-by-step directions included at the beginning of this book to teach students any necessary technology skills that they may not be familiar with.

2. Read the *Adding Titles Before and After a Clip* step-by-step directions (page 20; page020.pdf).

3. Have each student secretly choose a state and bring in pictures of the state's symbols, motto, and slogan. You may want to print out a list of these symbols and slogans for the class

Procedure

1. Write *Empire State*, *Golden State*, and *Lone Star State* on the board. Ask students if they know which states are known by these nicknames. Write *New York*, *California*, and *Texas* on the board. New York is called the Empire State because of its wealth during the early 1900s. California is called the Golden State because of the gold rush. Texas is the Lone Star State because of the single star on its state flag. If you are not teaching in the United States, you can use examples from your own country's regions.

Procedure *(cont.)*

2. Explain that each state or region has a history. Virginia is sometimes known as the Mother of Presidents because eight presidents were born there (more than any other state). It also received its name from the Queen of England, who was sometimes called the Virgin Queen.

3. Have students share the symbols, mottoes, and slogans they have brought in from home. Can their classmates guess the states represented by these clues?

4. Tell students they will be making movies about state symbols, slogans, and mottoes. For these movies, they will need to have at least eight pictures or video clips that show different state symbols, slogans, and mottoes.

5. If students have not brought in information on their chosen states, give them time to research the symbols, slogans, and mottoes of the states. Have them work in pairs. If two students brought in the same state's items, they can work together. Otherwise, they will need to pick one state to use.

6. Explain to students that they will need to make storyboards before they can make their movies. Have them start thinking of titles for their movies. Distribute copies of the storyboard template available on the CD (storyboard01.doc). Give students time to work on their storyboards using the information they have gathered.

7. Explain to students that, in this lesson, they are going to learn how to add titles before and after clips. Explain that adding a title before a scene is a good way to introduce a new scene. Adding a title after a clip is a good way to review a scene or to introduce the next scene. Having titles before and after clips is a great way to include important information.

8. Have students capture and import any still images or videos they have to date. Remind the students to save their work.

9. Explain to students that they should continue to research their chosen states. Remind them that the more material they have to work with, the more editing choices they will have. It is better to have too many choices than not enough.

10. Review the rubric (page 55) with students so that they understand how their work will be assessed.

Extension Idea

Have students interview two or three people from different states or people who have been to other states. Videotape them talking about their state flowers, birds, and mottoes. Ask them what the states' reasons were for choosing the symbols.

Student Directions *Movie Maker*

1. Click **Show Storyboard**.
2. Click on the clip that will be before or after your new title.
3. Click **Tools** on the Menu bar.
4. Click ***Titles and Credits...***.
5. Click *Add title before the selected clip* or *Add title after the selected clip*.
6. Type the words you want in the title.
7. Click *Change the text font and color.*
8. Click *Change the title animation.*
9. Click *Done, add title to movie.*
10. Your title clip is added.
11. Click the **Play** button to preview the title in the Monitor pane.

Assessment Rubric

Strong (3 points)	Students' work includes at least 8 photographs or video clips depicting a state's symbols, motto, and slogan.	Storyboard is complete and shows great detail. Titles are used and are pertinent to the concept.	Students' work shows a strong understanding of the lesson objectives.
Effective (2 points)	Students' work includes 6–7 photographs or video clips depicting a state's symbols, motto, and slogan.	Storyboard is complete but could include more detail. Title is chosen for the movie, but few other titles are used.	Students' work shows an understanding of the lesson objectives.
Emerging (1 point)	Students' work includes 4–5 photographs or video clips depicting a state's symbols, motto, and slogan.	Storyboard is complete, but includes little detail. Title is chosen for the movie, but no other titles are used.	Students' work shows an emerging understanding of the lesson objectives.
Not Yet (0 points)	Students' work includes 1–3 photographs or video clips depicting a state's symbols, motto, and slogan.	Storyboard is incomplete. No titles were chosen for the movie.	Students' work shows a weak understanding of the lesson objectives.
Self Score			
Teacher Score			
Total Score			

Comments

My State in Timeline

Lesson Description

Students will learn how to work with audio tracks that they have recorded with the video camera. Students will learn how to use Timeline View(er).

Content Standard

Students will understand how symbols, slogans, and mottoes represent the states.

Technology Skill

Students work with audio tracks.

Additional Technology Skills

- saving work
- capturing and importing video
- adding titles
- using Timeline View(er)

Materials

- digital camera
- video camera

Teacher Preparation

1. Use the step-by-step directions included at the beginning of this book to teach students any necessary technology skills that they may not be familiar with.

2. Read the *Working with Audio* step-by-step directions (pages 21–22; page021.pdf). These directions include how to import an audio file and how to work with Timeline View or Timeline Viewer.

3. Record at least two sample videos with audio so that students can see what is expected. One sample should be clear and set in a quiet background. The other sample should be taped in a noisy area so students can see how noise interferes with the audio.

Procedure

1. Remind students of the previous lesson about the states (*States and Their Symbols*). This lesson is a continuation of that lesson.

2. Share the sample video clips with the class. Ask if the video clips are clear. Ask if the students can understand what is being said. Can they hear any background noise that interferes with their enjoyment of each video? Do they think including audio would help or hurt their movies?

Procedure *(cont.)*

3. Explain to students that this lesson covers how to work with audio tracks. Tell them that they will be using video cameras to record someone talking about the states they chose. Students can tape themselves, their partners, find someone in the school who is willing to be taped, or they can tape people at home. The taping can be done in whatever style the student chooses—maybe in interview fashion or just a recital of the facts. Many video cameras today have built-in microphones. Explain to the students that, when they record audio, they should be very careful and aware of background noise. They should try to record the audio in a quiet place.

4. Help students shoot at least three video clips so they can have choices for editing. After taping, students can decide which audio clips should be included in their movies.

5. Explain to students that, in this lesson, they will learn how to work with audio tracks using Timeline View(er). Model for students how to use Timeline View(er). While Timeline View(er) is very similar to Storyboard View or Clip Viewer, it is more concerned with time and the sequence of the movie.

6. Have students brainstorm with their partners other state symbols that they may not have thought of yet. For example, they could choose state quarters and state nicknames. Challenge them to find out more interesting facts about their states for the next lesson. Give the students time to capture and import any new video or still images they have made.

7. Have students update their storyboards to include any new images or titles. Remind them that keeping their storyboards current will help them to stay organized.

8. Review the rubric (page 59) with students so that they understand how their work will be assessed.

9. Tell students that for their next lesson, they will learn how to work with music. Ask them to bring in at least four pieces of music they think will be great additions to their movies. Suggest to them that using a state song like "Georgia on my Mind" would be a great way to tie the pieces of their movies together. Make sure they have parent permission before they bring in any CDs.

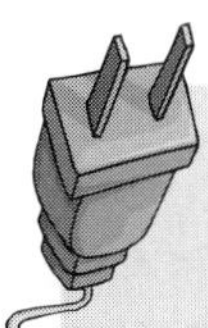

Extension Idea

Have students experiment with sound effects. Sound effects are another layer of audio that can add interest to the overall productions.

Student Directions *Movie Maker*

1. Go to the Collections pane. Click on the collection where you want to put your new audio file.
2. Click **File** on the Menu bar.
3. Click ***Import into Collections***.
4. Your teacher will help you find your audio file. Click to select the audio file.
5. Click **Import**.
6. The audio file is added to your collection.
7. Next, it's time to put the audio file in your movie! Click on the audio file. Hold down the mouse button. Then, drag the audio clip to where you want it in the Audio or Music track in the Timeline.
8. The audio clip is added to your movie.
9. Save your work.

Assessment Rubric

Strong (3 points)	Students videotaped at least three clips for their movie.	Video clips support the content of the movie. Audio is clear with little background noise.	Students experimented with editing choices while in Timeline View(er).	Students' work shows a strong understanding of the lesson objectives.
Effective (2 points)	Students videotaped two clips for their movie.	Video clips support the content of the movie. Audio is clear but has some background noise.	Students successfully imported at least one video clip into Timeline View(er).	Students' work shows an understanding of the lesson objectives.
Emerging (1 point)	Students videotaped one clip for their movie.	Video clips support the content of the movie. The sound is interrupted by background noise.	Students successfully imported video clips into Timeline View(er) but needed assistance.	Students' work shows an emerging understanding of the lesson objectives.
Not Yet (0 points)	Students did not videotape any clips.	Students had no clips to include in the movie.	Students were unable to work in Timeline View(er).	Students' work shows a weak understanding of the lesson objectives.
Self Score				
Teacher Score				
Total Score				
Comments				

My State's Music

Lesson Description

Students will learn how to work with music tracks.

Content Standard

Students will understand how symbols, slogans, and mottoes represent the states.

Technology Skill

Students work with music tracks and add them to their movies.

Additional Technology Skills

- saving work
- capturing and importing video or audio
- using Storyboard View or Clip Viewer
- using Timeline View or Timeline Viewer

Materials

- digital camera
- video camera
- CDs, cassettes, or digital songs

Teacher Preparation

1. Use the step-by-step directions included at the beginning of this book to teach students any necessary technology skills that they may not be familiar with.
2. Read the lesson, review the *Working with Music* step-by-step directions (page 23; page023.pdf).
3. Remind students that in the previous lesson they were asked to research at least four music choices for their movies. Have them bring these choices to school.

Procedure

1. Remind students of the previous lessons about the states (*States and Their Symbols* and *My State in Timeline*). This lesson is a continuation of those lessons.
2. Ask students if they have any new photographs or videos they would like to add to their projects and share with the class.
3. Have students share the music tracks they have brought to school to put in their movies. Make a guessing game about which piece of music goes with each state.
4. Explain to students that, in this lesson, they will learn how to add music tracks to their movies.

Procedure *(cont.)*

5. Demonstrate working with audio. In the Movie Tasks pane, click **Import audio or music**. Go to the folder where your audio file is located. Under Files of type, make sure *Audio and Music files* is selected. Click the desired audio file. Click **Import**. The audio file imports. The audio file appears in the Contents pane.

6. Ask students if the music tracks support and/or enhance their stories. Do they move the story along? Are they too quick or too slow? Do they distract or add to the overall production?

7a. Model for students how to open their saved work. Start *Movie Maker*. Click **File** on the Menu bar. Click ***Open Project***. Go to the folder where your project is saved. Click the project you want to open. Click **Open**. Show a student's saved project.

7b. If using a Macintosh, start *iMovie*. Click **File**; click ***Open Project***. Go to the folder where your project is saved, click the project you want to open, and click **Open**.

8. Review the directions for using Timeline View(er).

9. Work with students to import all of the music tracks they have selected. Having more options will help in the editing phase.

10. Remind students to save their work.

11. Review the rubric (page 63) with students so that they understand how their work will be assessed. Give the student pairs time to work on their projects. Be sure you also give them time to capture and import any new video or still images they have.

12. Have students update their storyboards to include any new images or titles. Remind the students that keeping their storyboards current will help them stay organized.

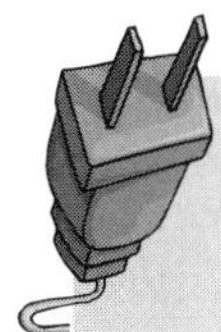

Extension Idea

Have students who play instruments record tracks to use in their movies.

Student Directions *Movie Maker*

If importing an audio file from a CD:

1. Have your teacher help you put the audio CD into your CD or DVD drive.
2. Click the **Audio** button. This will open the Audio pane.
3. The CD title will show in the pull-down menu.
4. Click on the song that you want. Hold your mouse button down. Drag the song from the Audio pane to where you want it on the Timeline.
5. The CD audio will be inserted in the Timeline.

If importing an audio file from iTunes:

1. Click the **Audio** button. This will open the Audio pane.
2. Your iTunes library is listed in the Audio pane.
3. Your teacher can help you click the pop-up menu. Choose your iTunes playlist.
4. If you cannot find the song, type a word or phrase in the Search field. The computer will look for the song.
5. Click on the song that you want. Hold your mouse button down. Drag the song from the Audio pane to where you want it on the Timeline.
6. The audio files from iTunes will be inserted in the Timeline.

Assessment Rubric

Strong (3 points)	Students experimented with at least four music tracks.	Students' chosen music tracks enhance and support the content of the movie. Music is creative and interesting.	Students' work shows a strong understanding of the lesson objectives.
Effective (2 points)	Students experimented with three music tracks.	Students' music tracks support the content of the movie.	Students' work shows an understanding of the lesson objectives.
Emerging (1 point)	Students experimented with two music tracks.	Students' music tracks support the content of the movie, but they could be more interesting.	Students' work shows an emerging understanding of the lesson objectives.
Not Yet (0 points)	Students experimented with one music track or no music tracks.	Students' music track does not support the content of the movie and, at times, is distracting.	Students' work shows a weak understanding of the lesson objectives.
Self Score			
Teacher Score			
Total Score			

Comments

My State Clips

Lesson Description

Students will learn how to work further with the clips they have chosen for their movies. They will learn how to rearrange clip sequences and delete clips from their movies.

Content Standard

Students will understand how symbols, slogans, and mottoes represent the states.

Technology Skill

Students rearrange and delete clips from their movies.

Additional Technology Skills

- saving work
- capturing and importing video
- using Storyboard View or Clip Viewer
- using Timeline View or Timeline Viewer

Materials

- digital camera
- video camera
- two video samples (video A is a completed sample; video B is the same as A, but its frames are out of order)

Teacher Preparation

1. Use the step-by-step directions included at the beginning of this book to teach students any necessary technology skills that they may not be familiar with.
2. Read the *Rearranging Clip Sequences and Deleting Clips* step-by-step directions (page 24; page024.pdf).
3. Before this lesson, review the directions from *Working with Clips* (page 16; page016.pdf).
4. If possible, prepare an example of a movie that has already been completed. Then, rearrange the sequence to demonstrate another choice. These sequences are called *video A* and *video B* in the procedure.

Procedure

1. Remind students of the previous lessons about the states (*States and Their Symbols, My State in Timeline*, and *My State's Music*). This lesson is a continuation of those lessons.
2. Play a completed movie (video A) for students. Then, play the same movie again with a different sequence of shots (video B). Ask the students which video works better, A or B. Why? Does changing the order of the shots help or hurt the message? Does the video become too choppy?

Procedure *(cont.)*

3. Explain to students that, in this lesson, they are going to learn how to work with the clips they have already captured and imported into their movies. They will learn how to take these clips, change the order, and delete some if necessary.
4. Model for students how to rearrange and delete clips. You can rearrange or delete clips while in Timeline View(er), Storyboard View, or Clip Viewer.
5. Work with student pairs to create different sequences of their movies by rearranging and deleting clips. Have them try at least three versions. Give them time to work on this process. Then, have students decide which version works best.
6. Tell students that in the next lesson they will be finishing their movies. This will be their last chance to add any new photographs, videos, or music tracks to their projects.
7. Give students time to capture and import any new materials.
8. Have students update their storyboards to include any new images or titles.
9. Remind students to save their work.
10. Review the rubric (page 67) with students so that they understand how their work will be assessed.

Extension Idea

Have students look at their friends' movies out of order and see if they can rearrange them to make more sense.

Student Directions *Movie Maker*

Moving a Clip

1. Find the clip you want to move.
2. Click on the clip. Hold your mouse button down. Drag the clip along the Timeline.
3. When the colored bar is where you want your clip, let go of the mouse button.
4. The clip is in its new place.

Deleting a Clip

1. Find the clip you want to delete.
2. Right-click the clip.
3. Choose **Delete** from the pop-up menu.
4. The clip is deleted from your movie.

Assessment Rubric

Strong (3 points)	Students experimented with at least three different sequences.	Final sequence is strong and is visually appealing. All clips strongly support the project.	Students completed the work independently.	Students' work shows a strong understanding of the lesson objectives.
Effective (2 points)	Students experimented with two different sequences.	Final sequence is visually appealing. All clips are pertinent to the project.	Students completed the work with some support.	Students' work shows an understanding of the lesson objectives.
Emerging (1 point)	Students experimented with only one sequence.	Final sequence works. But, some of the clips are not pertinent and should have been edited out.	Students completed the work with a lot of support.	Students' work shows an emerging understanding of the lesson objectives.
Not Yet (0 points)	Students experimented with a different sequence by just deleting or adding a scene.	Final sequence is visually unappealing.	Students did not complete the work.	Students' work shows a weak understanding of the lesson objectives.
Self Score				
Teacher Score				
Total Score				
Comments				

My State's Movie Style

Lesson Description

Students will experiment with different AutoMovie or Magic iMovie styles and transitions to complete their movies.

Content Standard

Students will understand how symbols, slogans, and mottoes represent their states.

Technology Skill

Students will learn how to use different styles or transitions to complete their movies.

Additional Technology Skills

- using Timeline View or Timeline Viewer
- saving work

Teacher Preparation

1. Use the step-by-step directions included at the beginning of this book to teach students any necessary technology skills that they may not be familiar with.
2. Read the *Using AutoMovie or Magic iMovie* step-by-step directions (page 19; page019.pdf)
3. Read the *Selecting a Movie Style* step-by-step directions (page 25; page025.pdf).
4. Let students know that they will be finishing their movies. Explain that this will be the last opportunity for them to make any changes.

Procedure

1. Remind students of the previous lessons about the states (*States and Their Symbols, My State in Timeline, My State's Music,* and *My State Clips*). This lesson is the culmination of those lessons.
2. Explain to students that they will be finishing their movies today using AutoMovie or Magic iMovie. Remind them that while they have already used this technology, they will be taking it a step further in this lesson by experimenting with different transitions and styles. A transition is the way one scene goes into the other.

Procedure *(cont.)*

3. Have the students open and review their saved work. Remind them to look at the scenes, the music, the title fonts, colors, styles, and the sequence of their movies to see if there is room for improvement.

4. Give students time to make changes and select a movie style. Have them experiment with at least two different styles. Explain to the students why one style might work better than another.

5. Model for the student pairs how to review their whole movies. Make sure the Playhead is at the beginning of the movie. Click the **Play** button on the Monitor pane to play a movie.

6. Remind the students to save their work.

7. When the students have completed their movies, allow them to play their movies for the class.

8. Review the rubric (page 71) with students so that they understand how their work will be assessed.

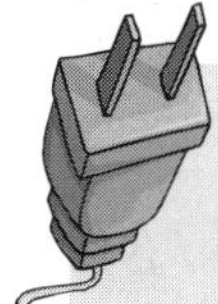

Extension Idea

Have the students complete similar movies using another history topic (perhaps a continent or region).

Student Directions *Movie Maker*

1. Click **Tools** on the Menu bar.
2. Click ***AutoMovie...***.
3. The AutoMovie wizard appears.
4. Select an AutoMovie editing style (see below).
5. Click *Done, edit movie*.

Types of Styles in AutoMovie

- **Highlights Movie**—This movie style has fast and slow transitions between clips. There is a title at the beginning of the movie. There are credits at the end of the movie.
- **Music Video**—This style matches the music. There are quick edits for a fast pace, and long edits for slower clips. The speed of the style is based on the music's beat.
- **Sports Highlights**—This style adds excitement to the movie.

Assessment Rubric

Strong (3 points)	Movie includes at least 8 photographs and/or video clips.	Movie is visually appealing, and the titles improve the presentation.	Transitions enhance the content of the movie.	Students' work shows a strong understanding of the lesson objectives.
Effective (2 points)	Movie shows 6–7 photographs and/or video clips	Movie is visually appealing, and titles were used.	Transitions somewhat enhance the content of the movie.	Students' work shows an understanding of the lesson objectives.
Emerging (1 point)	Movie shows 4–5 photographs and/or video clips.	Movie is somewhat visually appealing.	Some of the transitions enhance the content of the movie, while a few detract from it.	Students' work shows an emerging understanding of the lesson objectives.
Not Yet (0 points)	Movie shows fewer than 4 photographs and/or movie clips.	Movie is visually unappealing, and no titles were used.	Transitions detract from the overall flow of the movie.	Students' work shows a weak understanding of the lesson objectives.
Self Score				
Teacher Score				
Total Score				
Comments				

Saving the Planet One Step at a Time

Lesson Description

Students will learn how to use video effects in movies.

Content Standard

Students will know that living things are found almost everywhere in the world and that distinct environments support the lives of different types of plants and animals.

Technology Skill

Students use video effects in their movies.

Additional Technology Skills

- saving work
- capturing and importing stills or video
- working with titles and clips
- working in Storyboard View or Clip Viewer
- working with Timeline View or Timeline Viewer

Materials

- digital camera
- video camera
- K–2 storyboard template (storyboard01.doc)

Teacher Preparation

1. It is recommended that the Science lessons (pages 72–91) be taught as a unit so that students create completed movies. Use the step-by-step directions included at the beginning of this book to teach students any necessary technology skills that they may not be familiar with.
2. Review the *Using Video Effects* step-by-step directions (page 27; page027.pdf).
3. Bookmark Internet sites that are appropriate for students so they can perform further research.
4. Gather recycled and energy-saving items to be used as props for a scavenger hunt in the classroom. Some suggestions—empty water bottles, newspapers, magazines, empty aluminum cans, cardboard boxes, brown paper bags, glass containers, empty cartridges, and plastic jugs. Put some insulation around the windows and mark the light switch with an *X* to demonstrate some energy-saving ideas.

Procedure

1. Write these words on the board—*cans*, *plastic*, *newspaper*, *magazines*, *paper bags*, *cardboard*, *aluminum*, and *insulation*. Ask the students what all these words have in common. Send them on a scavenger hunt around the classroom to find items that can be recycled.

Procedure *(cont.)*

2. Have the students brainstorm other ways to help save the planet other than recycling. Some examples include: planting a tree, shutting off lights, switching to fluorescent light bulbs, bringing cloth bags to the market, using cloth napkins instead of paper, riding bikes, and taking shorter showers.

3. Tell students that they will be making a movie about things that can be done every day to help save the planet. For this movie, they will need to pick one idea and do a single storyline on that idea. Some suggestions could be recycling at home, recycling at school, or energy-saving tips. The movies should be between 15 and 20 seconds long.

4. Distribute copies of the K–2 storyboard template (storyboard01.doc). You may want students to work in pairs for this activity. Give students time to work on their storyboards. Direct them to be very detailed in their storyboards. Ask them to think about these details when putting their storyboards together. *Will there be any actors in your scenes; any props? What will your titles be? What kind of music will you be using?*

5. Explain to students that in this lesson they are going to learn how to work with video effects. Video effects let you add special effects to your movie. There are 23–28 video effects to choose from. Tell students that video effects should be used sparingly. Remind them that the focus should be on the contents and not on the effects. However, when used appropriately, video effects can add to and support the content.

6. Have students capture and import any stills or video that they have to date.

7. Have students experiment with different special effects on the scenes that they have captured and imported. Explain that some effects may work great while others will not work at all. Remind them to be careful that the special effects they choose do not take away from the focus of their movies.

8. Explain to students that they should continue to research their chosen ideas. Remind them that the more material they have to work with, the more editing choices they will have. It is better to have too many choices than not enough.

9. Tell students that in the next lesson, they will be learning how to record narration for their movies. This means they will need scripts. Have each student or pair of students pick one image that they want to import into the movie. For that image, each student should write a description. These will be the scripts for their narration.

10. Review the rubric (page 75) so that students understand how their work will be assessed.

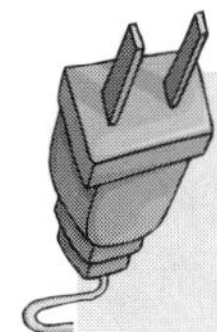

Extension Idea

Have students create similar movies in black and white. Have them compare these movies to their movies in color. Have them see if one technique works better than the other.

Student Directions *Movie Maker*

1. Click **Collections**.
2. Click the ***Video Effects*** folder. This is in the Collections pane.
3. Pick a video effect you want to see. Double-click on that video effect.
4. The video effect will show in the Monitor pane. This is called a preview.
5. Pick a video effect that you like. Then, click on it. Hold down your mouse button. Drag the effect to a clip in your movie.
6. There is a little star on the clip. This is the effects icon. It will turn blue. That means the effect has been added.
7. You can also delete an effect. Find the clip with the effect that you want to delete. Right-click the Effects icon in the lower-left corner.
8. Click **Delete Effects**.
9. The star turns from blue to gray. This means the video effect has been deleted.
10. Save your work.

Assessment Rubric

Strong (3 points)	Student experimented with at least four different video effects. Effects chosen supported the concept.	Storyboard is complete and shows great detail. Titles are used and are pertinent to the concept.	Student's work shows a strong understanding of the lesson objectives.
Effective (2 points)	Student experimented with three video effects. Effects chosen supported the concept.	Storyboard is complete but could include more detail. Title is chosen for the movie, but few titles are used throughout.	Student's work shows an understanding of the lesson objectives.
Emerging (1 point)	Student experimented with two video effects. They somewhat supported the concept.	Storyboard is complete, but includes little detail. Title is chosen for the movie. No additional titles were chosen.	Student's work shows an emerging understanding of the lesson objectives.
Not Yet (0 points)	Student experimented with one video effect. It did not support the concept.	Storyboard is incomplete and shows no detail. No titles were chosen.	Student's work shows a weak understanding of the lesson objectives.
Self Score			
Teacher Score			
Total Score			
Comments			

Let's Save the Planet

Lesson Description

Students will learn how to record narration while in Timeline View or Timeline Viewer.

Content Standard

Students will know that living things are found almost everywhere in the world and that distinct environments support the lives of different types of plants and animals.

Technology Skill

Students record narration in their movies.

Additional Technology Skills

- saving work
- capturing and importing clips
- working with titles
- working with clips
- working in Timeline View or Timeline Viewer

Materials

- digital camera
- video camera

Teacher Preparation

1. Use the step-by-step directions included at the beginning of this book to teach students any necessary technology skills that they may not be familiar with.
2. Read the *Recording Narration* step-by-step directions (page 28; page028.pdf).
3. Remind the students to bring in their scripts.

Procedure

1. Remind students of the previous lesson about living things on the planet (*Saving the Planet One Step at a Time*). This lesson is a continuation of that lesson.
2. Have the students read their scripts aloud to each other. Have them practice a few times so that their reading is fluent when they tape themselves.
3. Explain to the students that, in this lesson, they will learn how to record the script that they have created. If possible, have a few parents available to help.
4. Model for students how to record their narration using Timeline View or Timeline Viewer.
5. Give the students time to record the narration. If time permits, have them do one or two takes. Try to help students be aware of the timing of their scripts to make sure their recordings do not get too long.

Procedure *(cont.)*

6. Give students time to capture and import any new video clips or stills they have to date, including the images about which they wrote their scripts.

7. After recording, have the students see how the words fit with the picture in Timeline View. They may need to space some words out, cut a word or two, or add some more pictures. All of this is part of the editing process.

8. Help the students update their storyboards to include any new images or titles. Remind them that keeping their storyboards current will help keep them organized.

9. Review the rubric (page 79) so that students understand how their work will be assessed.

10. Tell the students that in the next lesson they will continue to learn how to work with audio tracks. They will learn how to balance the audio between the Audio and Music tracks. These tracks include narration, audio from video clips, and music. Tell students to bring in a few pieces of music for the next lesson.

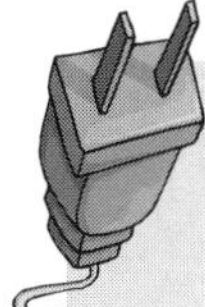

Extension Ideas

Have the students experiment with two different scripts for their movies. Have them record a male and female for each script. See which one works best.

Student Directions *Movie Maker*

1. Go to Timeline View. Drag the Playhead to where you want to start the narration. Your teacher can help you do this if you want.
2. Click **Narrate Timeline**. The Narrate Timeline dialog box will open.
3. Your teacher will help you watch your Input level. As you talk, your voice should stay in the green area. Do not talk too loudly. You do not want your voice to go into the red area.
4. Click ***Start Narration***. Begin talking. The program will play the video while you record. This way, you can make sure you are talking at the right speed.
5. When you finish, click ***Stop Narration***.
6. Type a filename for your narration. *Movie Maker* saves the file in a folder called *Narration*. This is in the *My Videos* folder with the rest of your clips.
7. Click **Save**.

Assessment Rubric

Strong (3 points)	Student's script completely explains the topic.	Student updated storyboard by including new video and audio.	Student successfully recorded the narration.	Student's work shows a strong understanding of the lesson objectives.
Effective (2 points)	Student's script mostly explains the topic.	Student updated storyboard by including almost all the new video and audio.	Student successfully recorded the narration, but some of the words could be clearer.	Student's work shows an understanding of the lesson objectives.
Emerging (1 point)	Student's script attempts to explain the topic.	Student did not completely update storyboard.	Student recorded the narration with a lot of help.	Student's work shows an emerging understanding of the lesson objectives.
Not Yet (0 points)	Student's script does not explain the topic.	Student did not update storyboard.	Student did not successfully record the narration.	Student's work shows a weak understanding of the lesson objectives.
Self Score				
Teacher Score				
Total Score				
Comments				

Let's Save the Planet—The Mix

Lesson Description

Students will learn how to adjust audio tracks while in Timeline View or Timeline Viewer. The audio tracks include narration tracks as well as the audio from any video clips they have imported.

Content Standard

Students will know that living things are found almost everywhere in the world and that distinct environments support the lives of different types of plants and animals.

Technology Skill

Students adjust the audio balance between the audio and the audio music tracks.

Additional Technology Skills

- saving work
- capturing and importing video or audio
- using Timeline View or Timeline Viewer

Materials

- digital camera
- video camera
- CDs or iTunes song list containing student music choices

Teacher Preparation

1. Use the step-by-step directions included at the beginning of this book to teach students any necessary technology skills that they may not be familiar with.
2. Read the *Adjusting Audio Balance* step-by-step directions (page 29; page029.pdf).
3. Make sure students have had a chance to gather some music choices together. Help them find music if they have not done so already.

Procedure

1. Remind students of the previous lessons about living things on the planet (*Saving the Planet One Step at a Time* and *Let's Save the Planet*). This lesson is a continuation of those lessons.
2. Divide the class into groups and have them share the music tracks they have selected. With their classmates' help, have each student choose a track for his or her movie.
3. Explain to students that in this lesson they will be learning how to balance the audio tracks in their movies. The audio tracks consist of music, voice-over narrations, and any audio associated with the video. Tell students that this is a very important step in the movie-making process.

Procedure *(cont.)*

4. Direct them to be careful that the music level does not overpower the level of the voice-over narration or audio from the video clips. It is important to hear what is being said. Tell students to be careful when doing this so that the music does not get too loud at any point.

5. For those who need it, model how to add audio from a CD or iTunes.

6. Ask students the following questions about the music they have chosen: *Does the music track support or enhance their story? Does it move the story along? Is it the correct pace? Does it distract from the overall production?*

7. Have students import the music tracks they have selected.

8. Then, have the students capture and import any new video they may have.

9. Demonstrate adjusting audio balance.

10. Give the students time to work on their project by adjusting the balance of the audio tracks. Have them experiment with adjusting the volume. Tell them to play all of the tracks together at least three times to make sure all of the sound can be heard. If time permits, have them play their audio mixes (a mix is when all the audio tracks are adjusted and work together as the final track) for the class.

11. Remind students to save their work.

12. Tell the students that in the next lesson they will be finishing their movies. This will be their last opportunity to add any video or make any changes.

13. Review the rubric (page 83) so that students understand how their work will be assessed.

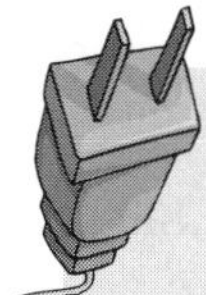

Extension Idea

Have the students create similar movies with different music tracks. This may require some re-editing of the pictures. Have them see if one version flows better than the other.

Student Directions *Movie Maker*

1. It is time to play with the volume of your clips.
2. Right-click an audio clip that has a volume you want to change.
3. Choose **Volume**.
4. Drag the slider to the left and right. This will change the volume.
5. Pick a volume that you like. Select **OK**.
6. You can also turn off all of the sound. This is called muting.
7. Right-click the audio clip you want to mute.
8. Choose **Mute**.
9. The sound is muted.

Assessment Rubric

Strong (3 points)	Music track enhances and supports the content of the movie. Music is creative and interesting.	Student successfully balanced the audio tracks by making sure all of the dialogue could be heard.	Student's work shows a strong understanding of the lesson objectives.
Effective (2 points)	Music track supports the content of the movie.	Student balanced the audio tracks, but at times the dialogue was difficult to hear.	Student's work shows an understanding of the lesson objectives.
Emerging (1 point)	Music track supports the content of the movie, but it could be more interesting and less expected.	Student somewhat balanced the audio tracks. Dialogue track was difficult to understand.	Student's work shows an emerging understanding of the lesson objectives.
Not Yet (0 points)	Music track does not support the content of the movie.	Student did not balance the audio tracks.	Student's work shows a weak understanding of the lesson objectives.
Self Score			
Teacher Score			
Total Score			
Comments			

Saving the Planet—The Movie

Lesson Description

Students will be finalizing their movie using AutoMovie or Magic iMovie.

Content Standard

Students will know that living things are found almost everywhere in the world and that distinct environments support the lives of different types of plants and animals.

Technology Skill

Students finalize their movies by choosing styles and transitions.

Additional Technology Skills

- saving work
- working with audio
- adjusting audio balance

Teacher Preparation

1. Use the step-by-step directions included at the beginning of this book to teach students any necessary technology skills that they may not be familiar with.
2. Read the *Producing the Movie* step-by-step directions (page 30; page030.pdf).
3. Remind students that they will be finishing their movies in the next lesson. That will be their last chance to make any final changes.

Procedure

1. Remind students of the previous lessons about living things on the planet (*Saving the Planet One Step at a Time*, *Let's Save the Planet*, and *Let's Save the Planet—The Mix*). This lesson is a continuation of those lessons.
2. Explain to students that in this lesson they are going to complete their movies using AutoMovie or Magic iMovie.
3. Have the students review their movies. You may want to ask some parents or other adults to come in and help students finish reviewing their movies.
4. Challenge students to see if they can make any improvements to the visuals first. Ask the following questions: *Do the titles help people understand the movie? Are the pictures interesting, or could they be better? Is the movie at least 15–20 seconds long?*

Procedure (*cont.*)

5. Then, have them move on to the audio part of their movies. Ask the following questions: *Can you hear the people talking? Can you understand every word that is being said? Does the music help the movie? Does the narration make the movie better?*

6. Give the students time to work on and finish their projects. Tell them to make at least one change that will improve their work.

7. Have the students share their completed movies with the class. Work with them to give praise and constructive criticism to their peers. The feedback they give to one another is very important.

8. Remind the students to save their work.

9. Explain to the students that the last step will be for them to share their movies with others.

10. Review the rubric (page 87) so that students understand how their work will be assessed.

Extension Idea

Pair each student with a partner. Have students perform peer assessments of the movies so that students can see where they need to make changes.

Student Directions *Movie Maker*

1. Click **Tools** on the Menu bar.
2. Click ***AutoMovie...***.
3. The AutoMovie wizard appears.
4. Select an AutoMovie editing style (see below).
5. Click *Done, edit movie.*

Types of Styles in AutoMovie

- **Highlights Movie**—This movie style has fast and slow transitions between clips. There is a title at the beginning of the movie. There are credits at the end of the movie.
- **Music Video**—This style matches the music. There are quick edits for a fast pace, and long edits for slower clips. The speed of the style is based on the music's beat.
- **Sports Highlights**—This style adds excitement to the movie.

Assessment Rubric

Strong (3 points)	Movie is at least 15–20 seconds long.	Movie is visually appealing, and the titles improve the presentation.	Audio tracks are well-balanced and enhance the content of the movie.	Student's work shows a strong understanding of the lesson objectives.
Effective (2 points)	Movie is 14 seconds long.	Movie is visually appealing, and titles were used.	Audio tracks are balanced and somewhat enhance the content of the movie.	Student's work shows an understanding of the lesson objectives.
Emerging (1 point)	Movie is between 10–13 seconds long.	Movie is somewhat visually appealing, and titles were used inconsistently.	Audio tracks are balanced but at times do not help the content of the movie.	Student's work shows an emerging understanding of the lesson objectives.
Not Yet (0 points)	Movie is less than 10 seconds long.	Movie is visually unappealing, and no titles were used.	Audio tracks are not well balanced and do not help the content of the movie.	Student's work shows a weak understanding of the lesson objectives.
Self Score				
Teacher Score				
Total Score				
Comments				

Let's Share Our Work

Lesson Description

Students will learn how to save and share their movies.

Content Standard

Students will know that living things are found almost everywhere in the world and that distinct environments support the lives of different types of plants and animals.

Technology Skill

Students share and save their work on recordable CDs and send them as email attachments.

Additional Technology Skills

- capturing and importing video or audio
- using Timeline View or Timeline Viewer
- working with AutoMovie or Magic iMovie

Materials

- recordable CDs
- Internet access and email address from which to send emails

Teacher Preparation

1. Use the step-by-step directions included at the beginning of this book to teach students any necessary technology skills that they may not be familiar with.
2. Either have students bring in their own recordable CDs, or purchase some for the students.
3. Read the *Saving the Final Movie* step-by-step directions (page 31; page031.pdf).

Procedure

1. Remind students of the previous lessons about living things on the planet (*Saving the Planet One Step at a Time*, *Let's Save the Planet*, *Let's Save the Planet—The Mix*, and *Saving the Planet—The Movie*). This lesson is the culmination of those lessons.
2. Review the rubric (page 91) so that students understand how their work will be assessed. This is the students' final opportunity to make any necessary changes to achieve the highest grade.
3. Explain to students that in this lesson they will be learning how to save and share their work. They will save their work on the computer as well as on CDs. They will also learn how to share their work via email.
4. Give the students time to review their completed movies and make any necessary changes.

Procedure *(cont.)*

5. At this point, have students watch their movies several times through to make sure the movies flow and do not need further editing. Let them find partners to assess their movies before showing the movies to the class or turning them in as completed projects.

6. Model for students how to save and share their movies.

7. Give students time to save their movies to CDs. Then, when students have finished their final edits, have them email their movies to you as attachments.

8. As a final activity, invite parents into the class to view these movies.

Extension Idea

Have students implement the environmentally sound strategies they shared in their movies.

Student Directions *Movie Maker*

Saving Your Final Movie to a CD

1. Click **Tasks**.
2. Under Finish Movie, click ***Save to CD***.
3. The Save Movie wizard will open. Type a filename for your movie.
4. You also need to type a name for the CD.
5. Click *Next*.
6. Click *Next* again.
7. It might take several minutes to save.
8. Click **Finish**.
9. Your movie is saved.

Saving Your Final Movie As an Email Attachment

1. Click **Tasks**.
2. Under Finish Movie, click ***Send in email***.
3. It might take a few minutes to save.
4. You might also want to save your movie on the computer. Click *Save a copy of the movie on my computer*.
5. Select *Next*.
6. An email will open. A new email is created with the movie attached.
7. Your teacher will help you type in an email address and a message.
8. Click **Send**.

Assessment Rubric

Strong (3 points)	Movie is at least 15–20 seconds long.	Movie is visually appealing, and the titles improve the presentation.	Student's work shows a strong understanding of the lesson objectives.
Effective (2 points)	Movie is 14 seconds long.	Movie is visually appealing, and titles were used.	Student's work shows an understanding of the lesson objectives.
Emerging (1 Point)	Movie is between 10–13 seconds long.	Movie is somewhat visually appealing, and titles were used inconsistently.	Student's work shows an emerging understanding of the lesson objectives.
Not Yet (0 Points)	Movie is less than 10 seconds long.	Movie is visually unappealing, and no titles were used.	Student's work shows a weak understanding of the lesson objectives.
Self Score			
Teacher Score			
Total Score			

Comments

Linear Patterns

Lesson Description

Students will capture and import still photographs and video footage that show the various ways patterns can be represented.

Content Standard

Students will recognize a wide variety of patterns and the rules that explain them.

Technology Skill

Students produce a shot list and storyboard and learn how to capture and import.

Additional Technology Skills

- using clip art
- saving work

Materials

- digital camera
- video camera
- sample pattern images (quilt.jpg; argyle.jpg; stripes.jpg)
- 3–5 storyboard template (storyboard02.doc)
- shot list template (shotlist.doc)
- pictures from home, newspapers, magazines, clip art, Internet
- video clips from home

Teacher Preparation

1. It is recommended that the Mathematics lessons (pages 92–111) be taught as a unit so that students create completed movies. Use the step-by-step directions included at the beginning of this book to teach students any necessary technology skills that they may not be familiar with.

2. A few days before this lesson, ask students to look for patterns that they can bring from home. Students might want to bring in fabrics that display patterns (for example, a quilt, an argyle sweater, or striped towel).

3. In addition, ask students to bring in pictures from home, school, or the Internet that show patterns. Challenge them to videotape as many of these images as possible.

4. Read the *Capturing and Importing Images* step-by-step directions (page 15; page015.pdf).

Procedure

1. Ask the students to name different patterns they see in the classroom. Have them share the items, pictures, and videos they brought from home. Show students the sample pattern images provided on the CD (quilt.jpg, argyle.jpg, stripes.jpg).

2. Write the words *linear patterns* on the board. See if any students can define linear patterns.

Procedure *(cont.)*

3. Depending on the patterns that students bring in, you might be able to say that many of these patterns are linear patterns. Explain that linear patterns are patterns that repeat indefinitely in either direction. This means that these patterns repeat over and over. Students can take another look at their patterns to see if they are linear patterns.

4. Tell students they will be making a movie about patterns. For this movie, they will need at least 12 still photographs or video clips that show different types of patterns. They might be able to use the items they brought from home.

5. Explain to students that before they can make movies, they must first create a shot list and storyboard. A shot list is a listing of the planned shots or scenes in the movie. A shot list is a good way to stay organized and will help with the storyboard.

6. Distribute copies of the the shot list template (shotlist.doc) and storyboard template (storyboard02.doc) to students. Give students time to work on their shot lists and storyboards.

7. Then, students should research and gather as many patterns for their storyboards as possible using clip art, magazines, digital cameras, video cameras, and the Internet.

8. Explain to students that in this lesson they are going to learn how to capture and import the photographs and videos they take. These images need to be neatly organized, captured, and imported into the proper folder. Demonstrate this by reviewing the *Capturing and Importing Images* step-by-step directions (page 15; page015.pdf).

9. Show students how and where to save their work.

10. Explain to students that this is the first step in the process of making their movies. They should continue looking for different types of patterns. Remind students that the more material they have to work with, the more editing choices they will have. Tell them that it is better to have too many choices than not enough.

11. Review the rubric (page 95) with students so that they understand how their work will be assessed. Give students time to work on their projects.

12. Before class ends, write the words *growing patterns* on the board. Give students several examples of growing patterns. Tell students to be on the lookout for these types of patterns and to bring them to the next class.

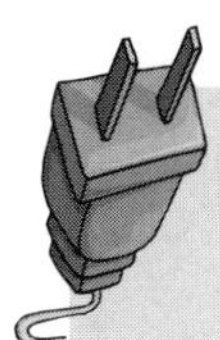

Extension Idea

Have students videotape classmates or siblings performing patterns using musical instruments.

Student Directions *Movie Maker*

1. Click the **Start** menu.
2. Point to ***All Programs***.
3. Click *Windows Movie Maker*.
4. If a new movie does not open, click **File** on the Menu bar. Click ***New Project***.
5. A new *Movie Maker* project opens.
6. To import an existing picture file click ***Import pictures*** in the Movie Tasks pane.
7. Ask your teacher to help you find the folder where your picture file is located.
8. Under Files of type, make sure *Picture Files* is selected.
9. Click the picture files that you want to put in your movie.
10. Click **Import**.
11. The picture files import.
12. The picture files appear in the Collections pane.
13. Save your work.

Assessment Rubric

Strong (3 points)	Student's work includes at least 12 photographs and/or video clips depicting patterns.	Shot list and storyboard are complete and show great detail.	Imported video clips contain focused content that supports the project.	Student's work shows a strong understanding of the lesson objectives.
Effective (2 points)	Student's work includes 8–11 photographs and/or video clips depicting patterns	Shot list and storyboard are complete but could include more detail.	Imported video clips support the project.	Student's work shows an understanding of the lesson objectives.
Emerging (1 point)	Student's work includes 5–7 photographs and/or video clips depicting patterns.	Shot list and storyboard are complete but include little detail.	Imported video clips support the project. Some clips could be more focused.	Student's work shows an emerging understanding of the lesson objectives.
Not Yet (0 points)	Student's work includes 0–4 photographs and/or video clips depicting patterns.	Shot list and storyboard are incomplete, showing no detail.	Imported video clips do not support the project.	Student's work shows a weak understanding of the lesson objectives.
Self Score				
Teacher Score				
Total Score				
Comments				

Growing Patterns

Lesson Description

Students will learn to work with the clips they have already captured and imported that show various patterns.

Content Standard

Students will recognize a wide variety of patterns and the rules that explain them.

Technology Skills

Students view clips, rename clips, and add clips to their movies.

Additional Technology Skills

- saving work

Materials

- digital camera
- video camera
- 3–5 patterns clips sample (pattern02_clip.avi; pattern02_clip.mov)
- video clips that show growing patterns
- pictures or clips from home, newspapers, magazines, clip art, Internet that show patterns

Teacher Preparation

1. Use the step-by-step directions included at the beginning of this book to teach students any necessary technology skills that they may not be familiar with.
2. Read the *Working with Clips* step-by-step directions (page 16; page016.pdf).
3. A few days before this lesson, ask students to remember the words that were on the board at the end of the last lesson—*growing patterns*. Remind them to bring any materials that have growing patterns.
4. Have *The House that Jack Built* by Mother Goose on hand to read to the students.

Procedure

1. Remind students of the previous lesson about patterns (*Linear Patterns*). Ask them if they have new photographs or videos that show linear patterns to add to their movies. Tell students that they will learn about a new type of linear pattern today.
2. Read *The House that Jack Built* by Mother Goose. Ask students if they saw any kind of pattern in the story. They should be able to recognize the growing pattern.
3. Ask students to give other examples of growing patterns. Students might give examples of growing patterns with numbers (2 + 2 = 4; 4 + 4 = 8; 8 + 8 = 16; and so on).
4. Ask students to describe clips that can show growing patterns. Let students share and demonstrate their ideas.

Procedure *(cont.)*

5. Bring out the video camera and have students tape one another for their movies. Tell students they will be adding these clips, along with images of growing patterns, to their movies.

6. Review the new technology skill—working with clips. Show students the sample clip (pattern02_clip.avi; pattern02_clip.mov).

7a. Model for students how to open their saved work. Start *Movie Maker*. Click **File** on the Menu bar. Click ***Open Project***. Go to the folder where the project is saved. Click the project you want to open. Click **Open**. Show a student's saved project.

7b. If using a Macintosh, start *iMovie*. Click **File**; click ***Open Project***. Go to the folder where your project is saved, click the project you want, and click **Open**.

8. Give students time to review their projects and to capture and import new material. Remind the students that they will need at least 12 clips for their movies. Clips will be saved in the Collections pane. Collections are libraries that contain the pictures that they have imported. They can use and reuse items for the collections for the movies they create. The Collections pane is found under **File** on the Menu bar. (If you are using *iMovie*, clips will be saved in the Clips pane.)

9a. Model how to view a clip by clicking **Collections** and choosing the collection that contains the clip you want to watch. In the Contents pane, click the clip you want. When the clip appears on the Monitor pane, click the **Play** button.

9b. If using a Macintosh, click the **Clips** button to bring up the Clips pane. In the Clips pane, click the clip you want to watch. The clip appears in the Monitor window. Click the **Play** button to watch your clip. You can also drag the slider bar to move quickly through the clip.

10a. Model for students how to rename a clip. Right-click the clip you want to rename. Choose **Rename**. Type a new name for your clip.

10b. If using a Macintosh, double-click the clip you want to rename. Type a new name in the name field. Click **Set** and your clip is renamed.

11. Show students how and where to save their work.

12. Remind students that this is an ongoing project and that they should continue to look for different patterns to include in their movies.

13. Review the rubric (page 99) with students so that they understand how their work will be assessed. Give students time to work on their projects.

14. Before class ends, write *repeating patterns* on the board. Tell students to be on the lookout for these types of patterns and bring them to the next class.

Extension Idea

Have students write their own growing pattern story. They can use *The House that Jack Built* as a model.

Student Directions *Movie Maker*

1. To import a video from a camera, turn the camera on. Connect it to the computer with a FireWire.
2. Set the camera to VTR mode. (Some cameras call this Play or VCR.)
3. In the Movie Tasks pane, click **Capture from the video device**.
4. Type a filename for your file. Choose a place to save your video file. Click **Next**.
5. Select ***Digital Device Format*** as the Video Setting. Click **Next**.
6. Select the Capture Method to capture parts of the tape manually. Click **Next**.
7. Use the DV camera controls to locate the beginning of the video you want to capture.
8. Select ***Start Capture*** to begin recording from the video.
9. Select ***Stop Capture*** to stop recording from the video.
10. Click **Finish** to close the Video Capture wizard.
11. Your captured clip is imported into the collection in the Contents pane.
12. Click the **Play** button to watch the clip. You can use the other Playback Controls to pause, stop, move forward or backward one frame at a time, fast forward, or rewind the clip.
13. To rename the clip, right-click the clip. Choose **Rename**. Type a new name for your clip.
14. Save your work.
15. Click, hold, and drag the clip down to the Timeline. As you move the clip over the Timeline, you will notice a vertical colored bar where it will be inserted if you let go of the mouse button.
16. When the vertical colored bar is visible where you want your clip inserted, release the mouse button. The clip is added to your movie. Include at least four new clips.
17. Save your work.

Assessment Rubric

Strong (3 points)	Student included at least four new clips for his or her movie.	All the clips the student has chosen depict patterns.	Imported video clips contain focused content that supports the project.	Student's work shows a strong understanding of the lesson objectives.
Effective (2 points)	Student included at least three new clips for his or her movie.	Most of the clips the student has chosen depict patterns.	Imported video clips support the project.	Student's work shows an understanding of the lesson objectives.
Emerging (1 point)	Student included one or two new clips for his or her movie.	Few of the clips the student has chosen depict patterns.	Imported video clips support the project. Some clips could be more focused.	Student's work shows an emerging understanding of the lesson objectives.
Not Yet (0 points)	Student did not include any new clips for his or her movie.	Not one of the clips the student has chosen depict patterns.	Imported video clips do not support the project.	Student's work shows a weak understanding of the lesson objectives.
Self Score				
Teacher Score				
Total Score				

Comments

Repeating Patterns

Lesson Description

Students will learn to take the clips that they have already captured and imported and add them to Storyboard View or Clip Viewer.

Content Standard

Students will recognize a wide variety of patterns and the rules that explain them.

Technology Skills

Students look at clips, arrange clips, and add or delete clips.

Additional Technology Skill

- saving work

Materials

- digital cameras
- beads and string for students to make necklaces or bracelets
- 3–5 patterns clips in order sample (pattern02_ordr.avi; pattern02_ordr.mov)

Teacher Preparation

1. Use the step-by-step directions included at the beginning of this book to teach students any necessary technology skills that they may not be familiar with.
2. Read the *Working in Storyboard View or Clip Viewer* step-by-step directions (page 17; page017.pdf).
3. A few days before the class begins, tell students that they will be making necklaces or bracelets using beads. The necklaces and bracelets will be formed using repeating patterns. Ask the students to bring beads from home, or purchase a few sets of inexpensive beads for the students to use.

Procedure

1. Remind students of the previous lessons about patterns (*Linear Patterns* and *Growing Patterns*). Today is a continuation of those lessons.
2. Give students piles of beads and pieces of string. Tell them to make patterns with the beads. It is best to have students string their beads so that the patterns will stay in place.
3. After a few minutes, ask students to describe their patterns. Some students may have included repeating patterns and others may have created growing patterns. Explain the difference.
4. Let students take pictures of these patterns to add to their movies.

Procedure *(cont.)*

5. Ask a student to tell about his or her favorite movie. After he or she has shared, ask students if the movie would have made sense if the end had come at the beginning and the middle was at the end. Most students will probably say that the movie would not make sense in that order.

6. Remind students that events in movies come in a certain order to make sense. The movies they make need to be in an order to make sense, too. Show students the sample provided on the CD (pattern02_ordr.avi; pattern02_ordr.mov). Tell students that they will be organizing and arranging the clips that they have already captured and imported with Storyboard View or Clip Viewer.

7. Explain that Storyboard View or Clip Viewer is the next step in the process of making their movies. Storyboard View or Clip Viewer shows the sequence of the clips in their movies.

8. Explain to students that with this technology, they will be able to put their clips in order, delete any clips that are not working for them, add any new clips they have, and arrange them in order for their movies.

9a. Model for students how to open their saved work. Start *Movie Maker*. Click **File** on the Menu bar. Click ***Open Project***. Go to the folder where your project is saved. Click the project you want to open. Click **Open**. Show a student's saved project.

9b. If using a Macintosh, start *iMovie*. Click **File**; click ***Open Project***. Go to the folder where your project is saved, click the project you want to open, and click **Open**.

10. Let students add any new clips or images to their movies and edit their movies using Storyboard View or Clip Viewer.

11. Remind students to save their work.

12. Review the rubric (page 103) with students so that they understand how their work will be assessed.

Extension Idea

Have the students tape their fellow students or friends in lines. Each student should be wearing a pattern. They will need to plan this activity by accessorizing the helpers. For example, #1 plaid shirt, #2 green hat, #3 blue jeans, #4 plaid shirt. While in line, students should have helpers alternate standing up and bending down.

Student Directions *Movie Maker*

1. To arrange clips, locate the clip you want to move.
2. Click, hold, and drag the desired clip along the storyboard. As you move the clip along the storyboard, you will notice a vertical colored bar where the clip will be relocated if you release the mouse button.
3. When the vertical colored bar is visible where you want your clip to be moved, release the mouse button. The clip will move to that position.
4. Find a new clip you want to add into your movie. These clips should be in your Collections pane.
5. Click, hold, and drag the clip down to the storyboard. As you move the clip over the storyboard, you will notice a vertical colored bar where the clip will be inserted if you release the mouse button.
6. When the vertical colored bar is visible where you want your clip inserted, release the mouse button. The clip will be added to your movie.
7. To delete a clip, find the clip you want to delete.
8. Right-click the clip.
9. Choose **Delete** from the pop-up menu.
10. The clip is deleted from your movie.
11. Save your work.

Assessment Rubric

Strong (3 points)	Student was creative in arranging the sequence in Storyboard View or Clip Viewer by experimenting with adding, deleting, and rearranging his or her photographs.	Student's work shows a strong understanding of the lesson objectives.
Effective (2 points)	Student experimented in Storyboard View or Clip Viewer by adding and rearranging their photographs.	Student's work shows an understanding of the lesson objectives.
Emerging (1 point)	Student experimented with Storyboard View or Clip Viewer by rearranging his or her photographs.	Student's work shows an emerging understanding of the lesson objectives.
Not Yet (0 points)	Student did not experiment with Storyboard View or Clip Viewer.	Student's work shows a weak understanding of the lesson objectives.
Self Score		
Teacher Score		
Total Score		

Comments

Giving Patterns Titles

Lesson Description

Students will learn how to add titles and credits to their movies. Students will also learn how to change the colors, fonts, styles, and sizes of their titles.

Content Standard

Students will recognize a wide variety of patterns and the rules that explain them.

Technology Skills

Students add titles to the beginnings of their movies and credits to the ends of their movies. Students change the colors, fonts, styles, and sizes of their titles.

Additional Technology Skills

- saving work
- using Storyboard View or Clip Viewer

Materials

- 3–5 patterns movie sample with titles and credits (pattern02_crdts.avi; pattern02_crdts.mov)

Teacher Preparation

1. Use the step-by-step directions included at the beginning of this book to teach students any necessary technology skills that they may not be familiar with.

2. Read the *Adding Titles and Credits* step-by-step directions (page 18; page018.pdf).

Procedure

1. Remind students of the previous lessons about patterns (*Linear Patterns*, *Growing Patterns*, and *Repeating Patterns*). Today is a continuation of those lessons.

2. Write a few of your favorite titles on the board. These titles can be of movies, books, or whatever you'd like. Tell students why you like these titles. Then, discuss some of the titles of their favorite movies or books to get them thinking about titles.

3. Write the word *pets* on the board. Brainstorm with the class what titles they think would work for a movie about pets. You could suggest *Hog Wild*. Once students come up with titles, explain that each of them will be creating a movie title. They will have to think creatively to come up with original titles for their movies.

Procedure *(cont.)*

4. Tell students that the text they add to the movie (wherever they choose to place it) can be a title. Titles can be added at the beginning, at the end, over an existing clip, and before or after a clip. For this lesson, they will learn how to add titles at the beginnings and ends of their movies. The titles at the ends of the movies are called *credits*. The credits tell about the people involved in making the movie.
5. Have the students work with partners to come up with creative, fun, and interesting titles for their movies.
6. Explain to the students that they will be adding titles and credits to their movies. Explain that they will also have opportunities to change the color, font, style, and size of their titles.
7. Show students the sample movie that is provided on the CD (pattern02_crdts.avi; pattern02_crdts.mov).
8. Give students time to open their projects, review their projects to date, and review their titles and credits.
9. Remind students to save their finished work.
10. Review the rubric (page 107) with students so they understand how their work will be assessed.

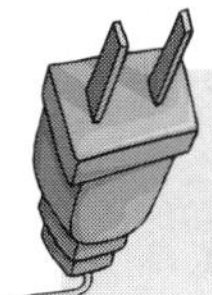

Extension Idea

Have students experiment with animating titles. Students can zoom into titles and then zoom out. Have the titles come in from the left side and leave off to the right side.

Student Directions *Movie Maker*

1. To add a title to the beginning of your movie, click the **Show Storyboard** button to display the storyboard.
2. Click **Tools** on the Menu bar. Select ***Titles and Credits...***. Choose *Add titles at the beginning of the movie*.
3. Type the text you want to include on the slide (for example, *Linear Patterns*).
4. Click *Done, add title to movie*. Your title clip is added to the beginning of the movie.
5. Click the **Play** button to preview the title in the Monitor pane.
6. To add credits, click **Tools** on the Menu bar. Select ***Titles and Credits...***. Choose *Add credits at the end of the movie*.
7. Type the closing text (for example, *Produced by: [your name]*).
8. Click *Done, add title to movie*. Your ending credits are added to the end of the movie.
9. Click the **Play** button to preview the title in the Monitor pane.
10. To change the style, color, or font, right-click the title or credits clip and choose **Edit Title...** from the pop-up menu.
11. In the Enter Text for Title pane, click *Change the text font and color*.
12. In the Select Title Font and Color pane, choose a different font from the Font drop-down menu.
13. Choose a style and color for your text.
14. To increase or decrease text size, click *Size options*.
15. Choose a position or justification for your text. You can align the text on the left, in the center, or on the right.
16. When the text attributes are set to your satisfaction, click **Done** to apply them to the titles or credits.
17. Save your work.

Assessment Rubric

Strong (3 points)	Movie includes an opening title and closing credits that accurately describe the movie.	Creative use of fonts, styles, colors, and sizes creates a visually appealing opening title and closing credits.	Student's work shows a strong understanding of the lesson objectives.
Effective (2 points)	Movie includes an opening title and closing credits.	Student was able to use font, style, color, and size applications in either the title or credits, but not both.	Student's work shows an understanding of the lesson objectives.
Emerging (1 point)	Movie includes either an opening title or closing credits, but not both.	Student used one of the font, style, color, or size applications.	Student's work shows an emerging understanding of the lesson objectives.
Not Yet (0 points)	Movie does not include titles or credits.	Student did not use font, style, color, or size applications.	Student's work shows a weak understanding of the lesson objectives.
Self Score			
Teacher Score			
Total Score			
Comments			

Patterns Around Us Movie

Lesson Description

Students will use AutoMovie or Magic iMovie.

Content Standard

Students will recognize a wide variety of patterns and the rules that explain them.

Technology Skill

Students pick styles and transitions for their movies.

Additional Technology Skills

- capture and import photographs or videos
- using Storyboard View or Clip Viewer
- saving work

Materials

- 3–5 patterns movie sample (pattern02_movie.avi; pattern02_movie.mov)

Teacher Preparation

1. Use the step-by-step directions included at the beginning of this book to teach students any necessary technology skills that they may not be familiar with.
2. Read the *Using AutoMovie or Magic iMovie* step-by-step directions (page 19; page019.pdf).
3. Let the students know that they will be finishing their movies. Explain to them that this will be their last opportunity to add any new materials to these projects.

Procedure

1. Remind students of the previous lessons about patterns (*Linear Patterns*, *Growing Patterns*, *Repeating Patterns*, and *Giving Patterns Titles*). Today is a culmination of those lessons.
2. Explain to students that they will be finishing their movies today by using technology called AutoMovie or Magic iMovie.
3. Go over how to use AutoMovie or Magic iMovie. Explain that AutoMovie or Magic iMovie is a shortcut for them in producing their movies. AutoMovie or Magic iMovie will build and edit their movies based on the clips and titles they have stored in Storyboard View or Clip Viewer.

Procedures *(cont.)*

4a. Model for students how to open their saved work. Start *Movie Maker*. Click **File** on the Menu bar. Click ***Open Project***. Go to the folder where your project is saved. Click the project you want to open. Click **Open**. Show a student's saved project.

4b. If using a Macintosh, start *iMovie*. Click **File**; click ***Open Project***. Go to the folder where your project is saved, click the project you want, and click **Open**.

5. Give students time to review their saved work and to capture and import any new photographs or videos. Have the students share any new pattern videos they have found.

6. Review how to add titles and credits and how to change color, font, style, and size.

7. Have the students review their movies two or three times to see if there are any changes to be made to the colors, fonts, sizes, or styles of the type. If so, have them make the changes.

8. Show students the sample movie provided on the CD (pattern02_movie.avi; pattern02_movie.mov).

9. Remind the students to save their work.

10. Review the rubric (page 111) with students so that they understand how their work will be assessed.

11. When the students have completed their movies, allow some to play their movies for the class.

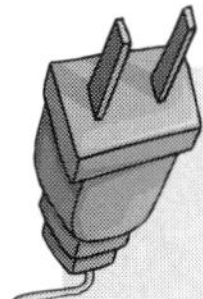

Extension Idea

Have students experiment with different AutoMovie styles. For this project, the other styles to experiment with are Flip and Slide (transitions include flip, slide, reveal, and page curl) and Sports Highlights (adds excitement with exploding titles, end credits that wrap around your video, fast pans, and zooms between clips). In *iMovie*, they can experiment with Random Choice.

Student Directions *Movie Maker*

1. Choose **Tools** on the Menu bar.
2. Select ***AutoMovie...***.
3. The AutoMovie wizard appears.
4. Select the ***Highlights Movie*** style.
5. Click *Done, edit movie*.
6. All your transitions and titling are added to the Storyboard.
7. Make sure the Playhead is at the beginning of the movie.
8. Click the Monitors pane **Play** button to play the AutoMovie.
9. Save your work.

Assessment Rubric

Strong (3 points)	Movie shows at least 12 pictures and clips that show patterns.	Movie is visually appealing, and the titles improve the presentation.	Student completed the work independently.	Student's work shows a strong understanding of the lesson objectives.
Effective (2 points)	Movie shows 8–11 clips or pictures.	Movie is visually appealing.	Student completed the work with some support.	Student's work shows an understanding of the lesson objectives.
Emerging (1 point)	Movie shows 4–7 clips or pictures.	Movie is somewhat visually appealing.	Student completed the work with a lot of support.	Student's work shows an emerging understanding of the lesson objectives.
Not Yet (0 points)	Movie shows 0–3 clips or pictures.	Movie is visually unappealing, and no titles were used.	Student did not complete the work.	Student's work shows a weak understanding of the lesson objectives.
Self Score				
Teacher Score				
Total Score				
Comments				

My Country

Lesson Description

Student will learn how to add titles before and after clips that they have already captured and imported in Storyboard View or Clip Viewer.

Content Standard

Students will understand how various holidays reflect the shared values, principles, and beliefs of people.

Technology Skill

Students add titles before and after clips.

Additional Technology Skills

- capturing and importing still images and videos
- using Storyboard View or Clip Viewer
- saving work

Materials

- digital camera
- video camera
- 3–5 storyboard template (storyboard02.doc)
- pictures and videos about holidays from home, newspapers, magazines, clip art, and the Internet

Teacher Preparation

1. It is recommended that the Social Studies lessons (pages 112–131) be taught as a unit so that students create completed movies. Use the step-by-step directions included at the beginning of this book to teach students any necessary technology skills that they may not be familiar with.

2. Read the *Adding Titles Before and After a Clip* step-by-step directions (page 20; page020.pdf).

3. Bring in books about holidays from the library. Bookmark Internet sites that are appropriate for students to perform further research.

Procedure

1. Begin the lesson by announcing to students that you are thinking of a national holiday. Tell students that you are going to give them clues so that they can guess the correct holiday. They should raise their hands when they know what holiday you are describing. Write clues for the holiday one by one on the board or overhead, pausing in between each one. In the United States, for example, you could write: *food*, *Wampanoag*, *harvest*, and *Pilgrims*. By the last clue, most students will have their hands raised. They will know that the holiday is Thanksgiving Day.

2. Ask students to describe how the holiday you chose reflects what people in your country believe as a nation.

Procedure *(cont.)*

3. Tell students that they will work in pairs. Each pair will be choosing a holiday to research. They will be making movies about their holidays. For each movie, the students will need at least 12 still images or video clips to show how and why the holiday is celebrated as well as the history of the holiday and its importance.

4. Give students time to research their holidays using books, interviews, and the Internet. Prompt them by asking each pair to research why we celebrate the holiday, what it means to our country, the history of the holiday, and how their families celebrate the holiday.

5. Distribute copies of the storyboard template (storyboard02.doc) to students. Give the students time to work on their storyboards. Remind them that storyboards detail the ideas for their video projects, including any stills, videos, text, and music that they will use. The storyboards will detail how the videos will convey their understanding of their holidays. Remind students that keeping their storyboards up-to-date will help keep them organized.

6. Explain to the students that in this lesson they are going to learn how to add titles before and after clips. Explain that adding a title before a scene is a good way to introduce a new scene. Adding a title after a scene is a good way to review a scene or to introduce a new one.

7. Have the students capture and import still images and videos as listed on their storyboards. Then, they can follow the student directions to add titles throughout their movies.

8. Remind students how to save their work.

9. Tell students that they should continue to research their chosen holidays. Remind them that the more material they have to work with, the more editing choices they will have. It is better to have too many choices than not enough.

10. Review the rubric (page 115) with students so that they understand how their work will be assessed.

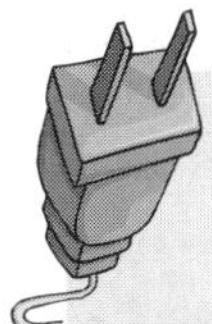

Extension Idea

Tell students that in the next lesson, they will be learning how to work in Timeline View or Timeline Viewer. Only in Timeline View(er) can you work with audio. To prepare for this lesson, have each student videotape a family member explaining how he or she remembers celebrating this holiday as a child. Ask them if the way we celebrate it today is the same or different. Many people will say they have carried on a tradition by celebrating the holiday in the same way every year. Some people will say they have established their own traditions and do it a bit differently than their parents did.

Student Directions *Movie Maker*

1. Click **Show Storyboard**.
2. Select the clip that you want your title to come before or after.
3. Click **Tools** on the Menu bar.
4. Click ***Titles and Credits...***.
5. Click *Add title before the selected clip* or *Add title after the selected clip*.
6. Type the text that you want in the title.
7. Click *Change the text font and color*. Choose a font and the color that you want the font to be. You can be very creative with your choices.
8. Click *Change the title animation*. This is where you get to decide how you want the title to appear. It can fly in, fade in and out, or just appear.
9. Select *Done, add title to movie*.
10. Your title clip is added.
11. Click the **Play** button to preview the title in the Monitor pane.

Assessment Rubric

Strong (3 points)	Work includes at least 12 photographs or video clips depicting the chosen holiday.	Storyboard is complete and shows great detail. Titles are used and are pertinent to the concept.	Students' work shows a strong understanding of the lesson objectives.
Effective (2 points)	Work includes 9–11 photographs or video clips depicting the chosen holiday.	Storyboard is complete but could include more detail. Title is chosen for the movie, but few other titles are used throughout.	Students' work shows an understanding of the lesson objectives.
Emerging (1 point)	Work includes 6–8 photographs or video clips depicting the chosen holiday.	Storyboard is complete but includes little detail. Title is chosen for the movie. No additional titles were chosen.	Students' work shows an emerging understanding of the lesson objectives.
Not Yet (0 points)	Work includes 0–5 photographs or video clips depicting the chosen holiday.	Storyboard is incomplete, showing no detail. No titles were chosen for the movie.	Students' work shows a weak understanding of the lesson objectives.
Self Score			
Teacher Score			
Total Score			
Comments			

My Country in Timeline

Lesson Description

Students will learn how to work with audio tracks that they have recorded with a video camera. They will learn how to work with Timeline View or Timeline Viewer.

Content Standard

Students will understand how various holidays reflect the shared values, principles, and beliefs of people.

Technology Skill

Students will learn how to work with audio tracks recorded with a video camera.

Additional Technology Skills

- capturing and importing video
- using Storyboard View or Clip Viewer
- working with titles
- saving work

Materials

- digital camera
- video camera
- pictures and videos from home, newspapers, magazines, clip art, and the Internet of holiday traditions

Teacher Preparation

1. Use the step-by-step directions included at the beginning of this book to teach students any necessary technology skills that they may not be familiar with.

2. Read the *Working with Audio* step-by-step directions (pages 21–22; page021.pdf). These directions include how to import an audio file and how to work with Timeline View(er).

3. Record at least two sample videos with audio so that students can see what is expected. One sample should be clear and set in a quiet background. The other should be taped in a noisy area so students can see how noise interferes with the audio.

Procedure

1. Remind students of the previous lesson about holidays (*My Country*). This lesson is a continuation of that lesson.

2. Share the sample video clips with the class. Ask if the video clips are clear. Ask if the students can understand what is being said. Can they hear any background noise that interferes with their enjoyment of the video? Do they think including audio would help or hurt their movies?

3. Explain to students that this lesson covers how to work with audio tracks. Tell student pairs that they will be using video cameras to record someone talking about the holidays they chose. Students can tape themselves, their partners, find someone in the school who is willing to be taped, or tape people at home.

Procedure *(cont.)*

4. Tell students that the taping can be done in whatever style they choose—maybe in interview fashion or just a recital of the facts. Many video cameras today have built-in microphones. Explain to the students that when they record audio, they should be very careful and aware of background noise. They should try to record the audio in a quiet place.

5. Give students time to shoot at least three video clips so they can have choices for editing. After taping, students can decide which audio clip(s) should be included in their movies.

6. Explain to students that in this lesson they will learn how to work with audio tracks using Timeline View or Timeline Viewer. Model for students how to use Timeline View(er) to import and work with audio clips.

7. Give the students time to capture and import the new videos or still images they have. Challenge students to find at least one more unusual fact about their holidays—something they themselves did not even know. For example, why does a certain holiday change its date every year? The facts are endless.

8. Have students update their storyboards to include any new images or titles. Remind them that keeping their storyboards and shot lists current will help them stay organized. Remind them to include their new video clips in their storyboards.

9. Review the rubric (page 119) with students so that they understand how their work will be assessed.

10. Tell students that for their next lesson they will learn how to work with music. Ask them to bring in at least four pieces of music they think will be great additions to their movies. Tell them that sometimes using a piece of music that is unexpected makes the movie more interesting, like using a contemporary jazz piece over a Thanksgiving dinner table. At other times, using an expected piece of music, like patriotic music for Veterans Day, works just great. Have them experiment with both types of music.

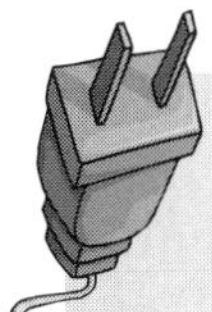

Extension Idea

Have the students experiment with sound effects by recording their own. Recording sound effects with household items is fun. For example, putting popcorn kernels in a water bottle and shaking it, scratching tape on a piece of clothing, or using their voices in unique ways. Just about anything works as a sound effect when used in the right place. Sound effects are another layer of audio that add interest to the overall production.

Student Directions *Movie Maker*

1. In the Collections pane, select the collection where you want the audio file stored.
2. Click **File** on the Menu bar.
3. Click ***Import into Collections***.
4. Choose the folder that contains the audio file you want to import. Select the audio file.
5. Click **Import**.
6. The audio file is added to the collection you chose in step 1.
7. Drag the audio clip to the desired location in the Audio or Music track in the Timeline.
8. The audio clip is added to your movie.
9. Click the **Set Audio Levels** button in the Timeline.
10. Drag the slider to adjust the audio balance. Dragging it to the right will increase the Audio or Music volume level while decreasing the audio from the video volume level. Dragging it to the left will do the opposite.
11. When you are done, click the **X** in the upper right-hand corner of the box to close the Audio Levels dialog box.

Assessment Rubric

Strong (3 points)	Students videotaped at least three clips.	Video clips support the content of the movie. The audio was clear.	Students successfully imported the video clips and experimented with editing choices.	Students' work shows a strong understanding of the lesson objectives.
Effective (2 points)	Students videotaped two clips.	Video clips support the content of the movie. Audio was clear, but there were some background noises.	Students successfully imported the video clips.	Students' work shows an understanding of the lesson objectives.
Emerging (1 point)	Students videotaped only one clip.	Video clip supports the content of the movie. Sound was interrupted by background noise.	Students successfully imported a video clip but needed assistance.	Students' work shows an emerging understanding of the lesson objectives.
Not Yet (0 points)	Students did not videotape any clips.	Students had no clips to include in their movie.	Students were unable to import video clips.	Students' work shows a weak understanding of the lesson objectives.
Self Score				
Teacher Score				
Total Score				

Comments

My Country's Music

Lesson Description

Students will learn how to work with music tracks.

Content Standard

Students will understand how various holidays reflect the shared values, principles, and beliefs of people.

Technology Skill

Students work with music tracks and add them to their movies.

Additional Technology Skills

- saving work
- capturing and importing video or audio
- using Storyboard View or Clip Viewer
- using Timeline View or Timeline Viewer

Materials

- digital camera
- video camera
- CDs, cassettes, or iTunes song list containing music choices

Teacher Preparation

1. Use the step-by-step directions included at the beginning of this book to teach students any necessary technology skills that they may not be familiar with.
2. Read the *Working with Music* step-by-step directions (page 23; page023.pdf).
3. Remind students that in the previous lesson, they were asked to research at least four music choices for their movies. Have them bring these choices to school.

Procedure

1. Remind students of the previous lessons about holidays (*My Country* and *My Country in Timeline*). This lesson is a continuation of those lessons.
2. Ask the students if they have any new photographs or videos that they would like to add to their projects. Have students share them with the class.
3. Divide the class into groups, and have students share their music tracks with their groups. With their classmates' help, have each pair choose a track for its movie.
4. Explain to students that in this lesson they will learn how to work with music tracks and add them to their movies.

Procedure *(cont.)*

5. Demonstrate working with audio. In the Movie Tasks pane, click **Import audio or music**. Go to the folder where your audio file is located. Under *Files of type*, make sure ***Audio and Music files*** is selected. Click the desired audio file. Click **Import**. The audio file imports. The audio file appears in the Contents pane.

6. Ask the students these questions: *Does the music track support and/or enhance the story? Does it move the story along? Is it too quick or too slow? Does it distract or add to the overall production?*

7. Model for students how to use Timeline View(er) to import their music.

8. In their pairs, have the students import all of the music tracks they have selected. Having more options will help in the editing phase. However, have them only place the one song they chose in the actual movie file. The rest can stay in the Audio pane.

9. Remind students to save their work.

10. Review the rubric (page 123) so that students will understand how their work will be assessed. Give the students sufficient time to work on their projects.

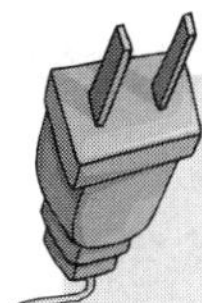

Extension Ideas

If any students play musical instruments, have them record tracks to use in their movies.

Student Directions *Movie Maker*

If importing an audio file from a CD:

1. Place the audio CD into your computer's CD or DVD drive.
2. Click the **Audio** button to bring up the Audio pane.
3. The CD title will appear in the pull-down menu.
4. Locate the song you want to import into your movie.
5. Drag the song from the Audio pane to the desired position on the Timeline.
6. The CD audio will be inserted in the Timeline.

If importing an audio file from iTunes:

1. Click the **Audio** button. This will open the Audio pane.
2. Your iTunes library is listed in the Audio pane.
3. Your teacher can help you click the pop-up menu. Choose your iTunes playlist.
4. If you cannot find the song, type a word or phrase in the Search field. The computer will look for the song.
5. Click on the song that you want. Hold your mouse button down. Drag the song from the Audio pane to where you want it on the Timeline.
6. The audio file from iTunes will be inserted in the Timeline.

Assessment Rubric

Strong (3 points)	Students experimented with at least four different music tracks.	Students' music track enhances and supports the content of the movie. It is creative and interesting.	Students' work shows a strong understanding of the lesson objectives.
Effective (2 points)	Students experimented with at least three different music tracks.	Students' music track supports the content of the movie.	Students' work shows an understanding of the lesson objectives.
Emerging (1 point)	Students experimented with at least two different music tracks.	Students' music track supports the content of the movie, but it could be more interesting.	Students' work shows an emerging understanding of the lesson objectives.
Not Yet (0 points)	Students experimented with one music track.	Students' music track does not support the content of the movie.	Students' work shows a weak understanding of the lesson objectives.
Self Score			
Teacher Score			
Total Score			
Comments			

My Country in Sequence

Lesson Description

Students will learn how to work further with the clips they have chosen for their movies. Students will learn how to rearrange a clip sequence and delete a clip from their movie.

Content Standard

Students will understand how various holidays reflect the shared values, principles, and beliefs of people.

Technology Skill

Students rearrange clips and delete clips from their movies.

Additional Technology Skills

- saving work
- capturing and importing video
- using Storyboard View or Clip Viewer
- using Timeline View or Timeline Viewer

Materials

- digital camera
- video camera
- two video samples (video A is a completed sample; video B is the same as A, but its frames are out of order)

Teacher Preparation

1. Use the step-by-step directions included at the beginning of this book to teach students any necessary technology skills that they may not be familiar with.
2. Read the *Rearranging Clip Sequences and Deleting Clips* step-by-step directions (page 24; page024.pdf).
3. Before this lesson, review the step-by-step directions from *Working with Clips* (page 16; page016.pdf).
4. If possible, prepare an example of a movie that has already been completed. Then, rearrange the sequence to demonstrate another choice. These sequences are called *video A* and *video B* in the procedure.

Procedure

1. Remind students of the previous lessons about holidays (*My Country*, *My Country in Timeline*, and *My Country's Music*). This lesson is a continuation of those lessons.
2. Play a completed movie (video A) for students. Then, play the same movie again with a different sequence of shots (video B). Ask the students which video works better, A or B. Why? Does changing the order of the shots help or hurt the message? Does the video become too choppy?

Procedure *(cont.)*

3. Explain to the students that, in this lesson, they are going to learn how to work with the clips they have already captured and imported into their movies. They will learn how to take these clips, change the order, and delete some, if necessary.
4. Model for students how to rearrange and delete clips. You can rearrange or delete clips while in Timeline View(er) or Storyboard View (Clip Viewer).
5. Have student pairs create different sequences of their movies by rearranging and deleting clips. Have them try at least three versions. Give them time to work on this process. Then, have students decide which version works best.
6. Tell students that during the next lesson, they will be finishing their movies. Tell them that they should review their movies before the next lesson to make sure they are happy with them. They will need to make any necessary changes before the next lesson, if possible. Ask the students if they have any new photographs, videos, or music tracks they would like to add to their projects. Tell students that this will be their last chance to add any new materials.
7. Give students time to capture and import any new materials.
8. Have students update their storyboards to include any new images or titles.
9. Remind students to save their work.
10. Review the rubric (page 127) with students so that they understand how their work will be assessed.

Extension Idea

Have students videotape friends putting on a play or a reenactment of their holiday. These videos could be a whole movie themselves.

Student Directions *Movie Maker*

Rearranging Clip Sequences

1. Find the clip you want to rearrange.
2. Click on the clip. Hold your mouse button down. Drag the clip along the Timeline. As you move the clip along the Timeline, you will see a vertical colored bar where it will be rearranged if you let go of the mouse.
3. When the vertical colored bar is where you want your clip rearranged, release the mouse button. The clip will be rearranged to that position.

Deleting a Clip from Your Movie

1. Find the clip you want to delete.
2. Right-click on the clip.
3. Choose **Delete** from the pop-up menu.
4. The clip is deleted from your movie.

Assessment Rubric

Strong (3 points)	Students experimented with at least three different sequences.	Final sequence is strong and is visually appealing. All clips strongly support the project.	Students completed the work independently.	Students' work shows a strong understanding of the lesson objectives.
Effective (2 points)	Students experimented with at least two different sequences.	Final sequence is visually appealing. All clips are pertinent to the project.	Students completed the work with a little support.	Students' work shows an understanding of the lesson objectives.
Emerging (1 point)	Students experimented with at least one sequence.	Final sequence works. However, some of the clips are not pertinent and should have been edited.	Students completed the work with some support.	Students' work shows an emerging understanding of the lesson objectives.
Not Yet (0 points)	Students experimented with a sequence by just deleting or adding a scene.	Final sequence is visually unappealing.	Students completed the work with a lot of support.	Students' work shows a weak understanding of the lesson objectives.
Self Score				
Teacher Score				
Total Score				
Comments				

My Country Movie

Lesson Description

Students will experiment with different AutoMovie or Magic iMovie styles and transitions to complete their movies.

Content Standard

Students will understand how various holidays reflect the shared values, principles, and beliefs of people.

Technology Skill

Students use different styles or transitions to complete their movies.

Additional Technology Skills

- using Timeline View or Timeline Viewer
- saving work

Teacher Preparation

1. Use the step-by-step directions included at the beginning of this book to teach students any necessary technology skills that they may not be familiar with.
2. Read the *Using AutoMovie or Magic iMovie* step-by-step directions (page 19; page019.pdf)
3. Read the *Selecting a Movie Style* step-by-step directions (page 25; page025.pdf).

Procedure

1. Remind students of the previous lessons about holidays (*My Country*, *My Country in Timeline*, *My Country's Music*, and *My Country in Sequence*). This lesson is the culmination of those lessons.
2. Get the students excited by letting them know that they will be finishing their movies. Explain that this is will be the last opportunity for them to make any changes.
3. Remind students that they have already used this technology. Now they will be taking it a step further by experimenting with different transitions or styles. A *transition* is the way one scene blends into another.
4. Go over how to use AutoMovie or Magic iMovie. Discuss different styles and transitions that are available in the programs.

Procedure *(cont.)*

5. Have the students open their saved work and review it. Ask this question: *Does the movie represent the holiday you studied?*

6. Remind student pairs to look at the scenes, the music, the titles (font, color, and style), and the sequence of their movies to see if there is any room for improvement.

7. Give students time to make any changes and select styles for their movies. Have them experiment with different styles to see which one works best. Explain to students why one style might work better than others. (In AutoMovie, if the music track is slow, a Highlights Movie might work best. If the music track has a fast pace, perhaps the Music Video style will work best.)

8. Model for students how to review their AutoMovie. Make sure the Playhead is at the beginning of the movie. Click the **Play** button on the Monitor pane to play the movie.

9. Remind students to save their work.

10. When students have completed the reviews of their movies, allow them to play their movies for the class.

11. Review the rubric (page 131) so that students understand how their work will be assessed.

Extension Idea

Have students complete similar movies from the point of view of one person. They can do this by interviewing the person and cutting back and forth between the interview and images of the holiday the person is sharing.

Student Directions *Movie Maker*

1. Click **Tools** on the Menu bar.
2. Click ***AutoMovie...***.
3. The AutoMovie wizard appears.
4. Select an AutoMovie editing style (see below).
5. Click *Done, edit movie.*

Types of Styles in AutoMovie

- **Highlights Movie**—This movie style has fast and slow transitions between clips. There is a title at the beginning of the movie. There are credits at the end of the movie.
- **Music Video**—This style matches the music. There are quick edits for a fast pace, and long edits for slower clips. The speed of the style is based on the music's beat.
- **Sports Highlights**—This style adds excitement to the movie.

Assessment Rubric

Strong (3 points)	Movie includes at least 12 photographs and/or video clips.	Movie is visually appealing, and the titles improve the presentation.	Transitions enhance the content of the movie.	Students' work shows a strong understanding of the lesson objectives.
Effective (2 points)	Movie includes 9–11 photographs and/or video clips	Movie is visually appealing, and titles were used.	Transitions somewhat enhance the content of the movie.	Students' work shows an understanding of the lesson objectives.
Emerging (1 point)	Movie includes 6–8 photographs and/or video clips.	Movie is somewhat visually appealing.	Some of the transitions enhance the content of the movie, while a few of them detract from it.	Students' work shows an emerging understanding of the lesson objectives.
Not Yet (0 points)	Movie includes at least five photographs and/or movie clips.	Movie is visually unappealing, and no titles were used.	Transitions detract from the overall flow of the movie.	Students' work shows a weak understanding of the lesson objectives.
Self Score				
Teacher Score				
Total Score				
Comments				

Our Environment—The Good, the Bad, and the Ugly

Lesson Description

Students will learn how various techniques, such as camera positions, camera angles, and sound quality, can help them make excellent movies. For this lesson, they will use these skills and begin making television commercials.

Content Standard

Students will know that all organisms (including humans) cause changes in their environments, and these changes can be beneficial or detrimental.

Technology Skill

Students learn various techniques, such as camera position and sound quality.

Additional Technology Skills

- saving work
- capturing and importing clips
- working with titles and clips
- working in Storyboard View or Clip Viewer
- working in Timeline View or Timeline Viewer

Materials

- 3–5 storyboard template (storyboard02.doc)
- copies of *Filming Techniques* (page 26; page026.pdf)

Teacher Preparation

1. It is recommended that the Science lessons (pages 132–150) be taught as a unit so that students create completed movies. Use the step-by-step directions included at the beginning of this book to teach students any necessary technology skills that they may not be familiar with.

2. Gather at least three TV commercials to review with the class. Tape these at home, or download them from Internet sites. If possible, find different styles for each. Some examples could include fast-paced or action commercials, talking-head commercials (one person speaking to camera), or simple commercials with titles only. Commercials with special effects or animation should not be used at this time.

Procedure

1. Explain to students that television commercials are used to market a product or an idea. Then play three commercials for the students. Ask the following questions: *What was the message or product in each commercial? Are these memorable commercials? Was there music? Were there titles? Were there logos or taglines?* Point out to students that there are many different types of commercials. Two elements that make a good commercial are a clear message and an entertainment value.

Procedure *(cont.)*

2. Tell students that they will each be making a television commercial about ways organisms help or harm the environment. It should demonstrate how the organisms of the universe cause changes to the environment. Some changes are harmful, and some are beneficial. Each commercial should be between 20–30 seconds long.

3. Brainstorm with the class some possible ideas for their commercials. For example, have students look at the way a lunch box is packed. What items are used in a lunch box that can harm or save the environment? (For example, using reusable water bottles, reusable containers, cloth napkins, and silverware all help the environment. Using plastic water bottles, plastic baggies, paper napkins, plasticware, and anything that must be thrown away all harm the environment.) Encourage students to think about ways to recycle and save energy at home, in school, and in their neighborhoods.

4. Distribute copies of the storyboard template (storyboard02.doc). and copies of *Filming Techniques* (page 26; page026.pdf).

5. As an exercise, have the students again review the commercials you brought. They should each pick one and do a storyboard for that commercial. Have them examine what types of shots are in the commercial (close ups, wide shots, long shots, pans, or zooms). Make note of these on the storyboard. Other things to describe in the storyboard are actors, props, different locations, notes on dialogue, and voice-over narration.

6. Remind them to add titles to their storyboard frames when titles are used. When there is music throughout their commercials, they should indicate this at the beginning of their storyboards by the words *music throughout*. Students should review their storyboards by comparing them to the finished commercial examples.

7. Have students start to work on their storyboards for their own commercials. Explain to them that they will be working on these commercials for a few lessons so that their storyboards will be continually updated as they gather more materials.

8. Tell students that they should continue to work on their projects by keeping in mind how to shoot the different camera angles, movements, and shots.

9. Review the rubric (page 134) so that students will see how their work will be assessed.

Extension idea

Have students research some other commercial examples. Have them find a non-humourous commercial. Then, ask students to explain how they would make the commercial humorous.

Assessment Rubric

Strong (3 points)	Commercial idea completely explains the concept.	Storyboard includes great detail.	Student's work shows a strong understanding of the lesson objectives.
Effective (2 points)	Commercial idea explains the concept.	Storyboard includes details.	Student's work shows an understanding of the lesson objectives.
Emerging (1 point)	Commercial idea somewhat explains the concept.	Storyboard is somewhat detailed.	Student's work shows an emerging understanding of the lesson objectives.
Not Yet (0 points)	Commercial idea does not explain the concept.	Storyboard is incomplete and shows very little detail.	Student's work shows a weak understanding of the lesson objectives.
Self Score			
Teacher Score			
Total Score			
Comments			

Our Environment—The Commercial

Lesson Description
Students will learn how to use video effects in their commercials.

Content Standard
Students will know that all organisms (including humans) cause changes in their environments, and these changes can be beneficial or detrimental.

Technology Skill
Students use video effects in movies.

Additional Technology Skills
- saving work
- capturing and importing
- working with titles
- working with clips
- working in Storyboard View or Clip Viewer
- working in Timeline View or Timeline Viewer

Materials
- digital camera
- video camera

Teacher Preparation
1. Use the step-by-step directions included at the beginning of this book to teach students any necessary technology skills that they may not be familiar with.
2. Read the *Using Video Effects* step-by-step directions (page 27; page027.pdf).
3. Bookmark Internet sites that are appropriate for students so they can perform further research.
4. Remind the students to bring in their storyboards.

Procedure
1. Remind students of the previous lesson about the environment (*Our Environment—The Good, the Bad, and the Ugly*). This lesson is a continuation of that lesson.
2. Have the students capture and import any new materials they have to date.
3. Give students time to review their storyboards. Have them update these, if necessary, to include any new information.
4. Explain to students that in this lesson they are going to learn how to work with video effects. Video effects let you add special effects to your movie. There are 23–28 video effects to choose from. Tell the students that video effects should be used sparingly. Remind them that the focus should be on the content and not on the effects. However, when used appropriately, video effects can add to and support the content.

Procedure *(cont.)*

5. Have students experiment with different special effects on the scenes they have captured and imported. Explain that some effects may work great while others will not work at all. Remind them to be careful that the special effects they choose do not take away from the focus of their commercials.

6. Remind students that they should continue to research their chosen ideas. The more material they have to work with, the more editing choices they will have. It is better to have too many choices than not enough of them.

7. Tell students that for the next lesson they will be learning how to record narration while in Timeline View(er). In order to record narration, students will need scripts. So, between now and the next lesson, they should each write a script to record. Give them time to write and revise these scripts.

8. Review the rubric (page 138) so that students understand how their work will be assessed.

Extension Idea

Have students complete similar television commercials where they are the "pitch people" for products. This is a good exercise in making sure the concept comes across in a creative way. For these new commercials, they should have classmates or friends videotape them selling or marketing their products.

Student Directions *Movie Maker*

1. Click **Collections**.
2. Click the ***Video Effects*** folder in the Collections pane.
3. Double-click the video effect you want to preview.
4. The video effect is previewed in the Monitor pane.
5. When you see one that you like, click on it. Hold down your mouse button and drag the desired effect to your chosen clip in the Storyboard or Timeline.
6. The effects icon star on the clip turns from gray to blue. That means that the effect has been added.
7. If you want to delete an effect after you apply it, you can. On the clip with the effect that you want to delete, right-click the Effect icon in the lower-left corner.
8. Choose **Delete Effects**.
9. The star turns from blue to gray and indicates that the video effect has been deleted.
10. Save your work.

Assessment Rubric

Strong (3 points)	Student experimented with at least four video effects. Effects chosen supported the concept.	Storyboard is updated and shows great detail.	Student's work shows a strong understanding of the lesson objectives.
Effective (2 points)	Student experimented with three video effects. Effects chosen supported the concept.	Storyboard is updated but could include more detail.	Student's work shows an understanding of the lesson objectives.
Emerging (1 point)	Student experimented with two video effects. Effects somewhat supported the concept.	Storyboard is updated but includes little detail.	Student's work shows an emerging understanding of the lesson objectives.
Not Yet (0 points)	Student experimented with one video effect. Video effect did not support the content.	Storyboard is incomplete and shows no detail.	Student's work shows a weak understanding of the lesson objectives.
Self Score			
Teacher Score			
Total Score			

Comments

The Voice of Our Environment

Lesson Description
Students will record narration while in Timeline View or Timeline Viewer.

Content Standard
Students will know that all organisms (including humans) cause changes in their environments, and these changes can be beneficial or detrimental.

Technology Skill
Students record narration for movies.

Additional Technology Skills
- saving work
- capturing and importing
- working with titles
- working with clips
- working in Timeline View or Timeline Viewer
- using video effects

Materials
- digital camera
- video camera

Teacher Preparation
1. Use the step-by-step directions included at the beginning of this book to teach students any necessary technology skills that they may not be familiar with.
2. Read the *Recording Narration* step-by-step directions (page 28; page028.pdf).
3. Remind students to bring their scripts to class.

Procedure
1. Remind students of the previous lessons about the environment (*Our Environment—The Good, the Bad, and the Ugly* and *Our Environment—The Commercial*). This lesson is a continuation of those lessons.
2. Have students review their final scripts, reading them a few times to see if there is any room for improvement.
3. Explain to students that in this lesson they will learn how to record the scripts that they have created. If the students would like, they can act like directors. To do this, have them choose classmates to be the voice-overs for their commercials. If they prefer to be the voice-over, they should have classmates help with the recording.
4. Model for students how to use Timeline View(er) to record their narrations.

Procedure *(cont.)*

5. Give students time to record their narrations. If time permits, have them complete one or two takes. If possible, be aware of the timing of the scripts and make sure they do not get too long or too short.

6. After recording, have the students see how the words fit with the pictures while in Timeline View(er). They may need to space some words out, cut a word or two, or add some more pictures. All of this is part of the editing process.

7. Give students time to capture and import any new video or stills they have to date.

8. Have students update their storyboards to include any new images or titles. Remind the students that keeping their storyboards current will help keep them organized.

9. Review the rubric (page 142) so that students understand how their work will be assessed.

10. Tell students that for the next lesson, they will continue to learn how to work with audio tracks. They will learn how to balance the audio between the audio and music tracks. These tracks include narration, audio from video clips, and music. Tell the students that they will need to have a selection of music for the next lesson.

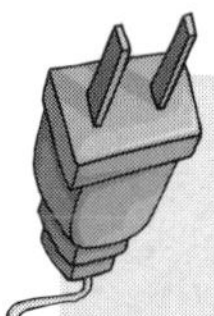

Extension Idea

Have students record a version of their commercials by recording two voices for the narration. For instance Voice A is the announcer and does the introduction or end tagline only (if there is one), and Voice B records the body of the script.

Student Directions *Movie Maker*

1. In Timeline View, drag the Playhead to the location where you want to start the narration.
2. Click **Narrate Timeline**.
3. In the Narrate Timeline dialog box, adjust the Input level. As you speak, your voice should fall into the green area and rarely or never go into the red.
4. Click ***Start Narration*** and begin speaking. Movie Maker plays the video while you record, allowing you to time your narration to the movie.
5. Click ***Stop Narration***.
6. Enter a filename for your narration. *Movie Maker* automatically saves the narration into a folder called *Narration*, located in the *My Videos* folder with the rest of your clips.
7. Click **Save**.
8. Your narration appears in the Timeline, beginning at the location you specified in step 1.

Assessment Rubric

Strong (3 points)	Script completely explains the topic.	Student updated storyboard by including new video and audio.	Student successfully recorded the narration.	Student's work shows a strong understanding of the lesson objectives.
Effective (2 points)	Script mostly explains the topic.	Student updated storyboard by including almost all of the new video and audio.	Student successfully recorded the narration, but some of the words could be clearer.	Student's work shows an understanding of the lesson objectives.
Emerging (1 point)	Script attempts to explain the topic.	Student did not completely update storyboard.	Student recorded the narration with a lot of help.	Student's work shows an emerging understanding of the lesson objectives.
Not Yet (0 points)	Script does not explain the topic.	Student did not update storyboard.	Student did not successfully record the narration.	Student's work shows a weak understanding of the lesson objectives.
Self Score				
Teacher Score				
Total Score				

Comments

Our Environment—Mixing Elements

Lesson Description

Students will learn how to adjust audio tracks while in Timeline View or Timeline Viewer. The audio tracks include narration tracks as well as the audio from any video clips they have imported.

Content Standard

Students will know that all organisms (including humans) cause changes in their environments, and these changes can be beneficial or detrimental.

Technology Skill

Students adjust the audio balance between the audio and the audio music tracks.

Additional Technology Skills

- saving work
- capturing and importing video or audio
- using Timeline View or Timeline Viewer

Materials

- digital camera
- video camera
- CDs or iTunes song lists containing their music choices

Teacher Preparation

1. Use the step-by-step directions included at the beginning of this book to teach students any necessary technology skills that they may not be familiar with.
2. Read the *Adjusting Audio Balance* step-by-step directions (page 29; page029.pdf).
3. Make sure students have had a chance to gather some music choices together. Help them find music if they have not done so already.

Procedure

1. Remind students of the previous lessons about the environment (*Our Environment—The Good, the Bad, and the Ugly, Our Environment—The Commercial,* and *The Voice of Our Environment*). This lesson is a continuation of those lessons.
2. Explain to the students that in this lesson they will be learning how to balance the audio tracks in their commercials. The audio tracks consist of music, voice-over narration, and any audio associated with the video. Tell students to be careful that the music level does not overpower the level of the voice-over narration or audio from the video clips as it is important to hear what is being said. If there is a break in the audio track, then the student can raise the volume of the music slightly to fill the hole.
3. For those who need it, model how to add audio from a CD or iTunes.

Procedure *(cont.)*

4. Ask students the following questions about the music they have chosen: *Do the music tracks support or enhance the content of the commercial? Do the songs move the story along? Is the music playing at the correct pace? Does it distract from the overall production?*

5. Have students import the music tracks they have selected.

6. Have students capture and import any new video they may have.

7. Demonstrate adjusting audio balance following the step-by-step directions.

8. Give students time to work on their commercials by adjusting the balance of the audio tracks. Have them experiment with adjusting the volume. Tell them to play all of the tracks together at least three times to make sure all the sound can be heard. If time permits, have them play their audio mixes (a mix is when all the audio tracks are adjusted and work together as the final track) for the class.

9. Remind students to save their work.

10. Tell students that in the next lesson they will be finishing their movies. This will be their last opportunity to add any video clips or make any changes.

11. Review the rubric (page 146) so that students will understand how their work will be assessed.

Extension Idea

Have students create similar commercials using different music tracks. This may require some re-editing of the pictures. See if one commercial gets the message across better than the others.

Student Directions *Movie Maker*

1. Right-click the audio clip that has a volume level you want to change.
2. Choose **Volume** from the contextual menu.
3. Drag the slider to adjust the volume.
4. Select **OK**.
5. If you would rather use Audio Balance, click **Set Audio Levels** in the Timeline.
6. Drag the slider to adjust the audio balance. Dragging to the right will increase the Audio or Music volume level while decreasing the Audio from Video volume level. Dragging to the left will do the opposite.
7. When you are done, click the **X** in the upper right-hand corner of the box to close the Audio Levels dialog box.
8. If you want to mute the sound, right-click the audio clip for which you want to mute the volume.
9. Choose **Mute** from the contextual menu.
10. The sound is muted.

Assessment Rubric

Strong (3 points)	Music track enhances and supports the content of the commercial. The music is creative and interesting.	Student successfully balanced the audio tracks by making sure all the dialogue can be heard.	Student's work shows a strong understanding of the lesson objectives.
Effective (2 points)	Music track supports the content of the commercial.	Student balanced the audio tracks, but at times, the dialogue was difficult to hear.	Student's work shows an understanding of the lesson objectives.
Emerging (1 point)	Music track supports the content of the commercial, but it could be more interesting and less expected.	Student somewhat balanced the audio tracks. The dialogue track was difficult to understand.	Students' work shows an emerging understanding of the lesson objectives.
Not Yet (0 points)	Music track does not support the content of the commercial and is distracting at times.	Student did not balance the audio tracks.	Student's work shows a weak understanding of the lesson objectives.
Self Score			
Teacher Score			
Total Score			
Comments			

Our Environment—The Finished Commercial

Lesson Description

Students will finish their commercials and learn how to save and share them.

Content Standard

Students will know that all organisms (including humans) cause changes in their environments, and these changes can be beneficial or detrimental.

Technology Skill

Students save and share their commercials on recordable CDs and as email attachments.

Additional Technology Skills

- saving work
- capturing and importing video or audio
- using Timeline View or Timeline Viewer
- working with AutoMovie or Magic iMovie

Materials

- digital camera
- video camera
- recordable CDs
- Internet access and email address from which to send emails

Teacher Preparation

1. Use the step-by-step directions included at the beginning of this book to teach students any necessary technology skills that they may not be familiar with.
2. Either have students bring in their own recordable CDs, or purchase some for the students.
3. Read the *Saving the Final Movie* step-by-step directions (page 31; page031.pdf).

Procedure

1. Remind students of the previous lessons about living things on the planet (*Our Environment—The Good, the Bad, and the Ugly*; *Our Environment—The Commercial*; *The Voice of Our Environment*; and *Our Environment—Mixing Elements*). This lesson is the culmination of those lessons.
2. Remind students of all their work on movie making. In these lessons, they learned how to work with titles, clips, music, and audio. They learned how to record narration and balance audio tracks.
3. Explain to students that in this lesson they are going complete their commercials using AutoMovie or Magic iMovie. Go over this technology, and make sure students are comfortable choosing styles or transitions.

Procedure *(cont.)*

4. Challenge students to see if they can make any improvements to the visuals first. Ask the following questions: *Do the titles help people understand the commercial? Are the pictures interesting, or could they be better? Is the commercial at least 20 seconds long? Do the images persuade people to help make the environment better?*

5. Have students move on to the audio parts of their commercials. Ask the following questions: *Can you hear people talking? Can you understand every word that is being said? Does the music help the commercial? Does the narration make the commercial better?*

6. Give students time to work on and finish their commercials. Tell them to make at least one change that will improve their work.

7. Have students share their completed commercials with the class. After all the commercials have been shared, have the students chose their favorite commercials.

8. Explain to students that they will now learn how to save and share their commercials on recordable CDs and as email attachments. Review the step-by-step directions on *Saving the Final Movie* (page 31; page031.pdf).

9. Give students time to save and share their work.

10. Review the rubric (page 150) so that students understand how their work will be assessed.

Extension Idea

Have students compare their finished commercials with favorite TV commercials. They can compare these commercials using Venn diagrams.

Student Directions *Movie Maker*

Saving Your Final Movie to a CD

1. Click **Tasks**.
2. Under Finish Movie, click ***Save to CD***.
3. In the Save Movie wizard, type a filename for your saved movie.
4. Type a name for the CD.
5. Click ***Next*** at the bottom of the window.
6. Click ***Next*** again.
7. Depending on the length of your movie, it might take several minutes to save.
8. If you want to save the movie to another CD, click the *Save the movie to another recordable CD* box.
9. Click **Finish**.
10. Your movie is saved.

Saving Your Final Movie As an Email Attachment

1. Click **Tasks**.
2. Under Finish Movie, click ***Send in email***.
3. Depending on the length of your movie, it might take a few minutes to save.
4. If you want to save a copy of the movie on your computer, click *Save a copy of the movie on my computer*.
5. Select *Next* at the bottom of the window.
6. Your email application opens, and a new email is created with the movie attached.
7. Type in an email address and a message.
8. Click **Send**.

Assessment Rubric

Strong (3 points)	Movie is at least 20–30 seconds long.	Movie is visually appealing, and the titles improve the presentation.	Audio tracks are well-balanced and enhance the content of the movie.	Student's work shows a strong understanding of the lesson objectives.
Effective (2 points)	Movie is 15–19 seconds long.	Movie is visually appealing, and titles were used.	Audio tracks are balanced and somewhat enhance the content of the movie.	Student's work shows an understanding of the lesson objectives.
Emerging (1 point)	Movie is between 10–14 seconds long.	Movie is somewhat visually appealing, and titles were used inconsistently.	Audio tracks are balanced but at times do not help the content of the movie.	Student's work shows an emerging understanding of the lesson objectives.
Not Yet (0 points)	Movie is less than 10 seconds long.	Movie is visually unappealing, and no titles were used.	Audio tracks are not well balanced and do not help content of the movie.	Student's work shows a weak understanding of the lesson objectives.
Self Score				
Teacher Score				
Total Score				
Comments				

Fibonacci Patterns

Lesson Description

Students will learn about Fibonacci numbers and how they show patterns.

Content Standard

Students will generalize from a pattern of observations made in particular cases, make conjectures, and provide supporting arguments for these conjectures.

Technology Skill

Students produce a shot list and a storyboard.

Additional Technology Skills

- using clip art

Materials

- video camera
- 6–8 storyboard template (storyboard03.doc)
- shot list template (shotlist.doc)

Teacher Preparation

1. It is recommended that the Mathematics lessons (pages 151–169) be taught as a unit so that students create completed movies. Use the step-by-step directions included at the beginning of this book to teach students any necessary technology skills that they may not be familiar with.

2. Be familiar with Fibonacci numbers and how they show patterns.

Procedure

1. Begin by writing this on the board: *1, 1, 2, 3, 5, 8, 13, . . .*

2. Challenge students to figure out what number will come next in the sequence. Most students will understand that the next number is 21. Ask students to define the pattern they see. *(When you add the previous two numbers, you get the next one.)*

3. Tell students that this sequence of patterns is called *Fibonacci numbers*. A mathematician who lived during the Middle Ages created the Fibonacci number sequence to explain how rabbits multiply. (If two adult rabbits in a cage had a pair of babies at the first of each month, how many rabbits would be in the cage at the end of a year, assuming that none of the rabbits die? It takes just one month for baby rabbits to become adult rabbits and breed.)

Procedure *(cont.)*

4. The smallest Fibonacci number is 1. When you add 0 to 1, you get another 1. So the sequence begins with 1, 1. The next number is 2 because the two previous numbers (1 and 1) added together is 2. The next number is 3 because the two previous numbers (2 and 1) added together is 3. The sequence continues infinitely.

5. Tell students that they will be working in pairs to make movies that show the Fibonacci sequence for the first 12 Fibonacci numbers. First, have students determine the first 12 Fibonacci numbers in the pattern. *(The answer is: 1, 1, 2, 3, 5, 8, 13, 21, 34, 55, 89, and 144.)* For their movies, they will need at least 12 still photographs or video clips that show the Fibonacci sequence, one for each of the 12 numbers.

6. Suggest to students that one way to develop their movies is by using single story lines. With a single story line, each pair of students would base its movie on one set of items. For example, a pair could show the Fibonacci pattern with marbles by beginning with a slide that shows one marble. The next slide would also show one marble, then two marbles, and so on. The final slide would show 144 marbles!

7. Explain to students that before they can make movies, they must first create shot lists and storyboards. A shot list is a listing of the planned shots or scenes in a movie. Storyboards show how the planned shots are arranged. They should decide what objects they will use to visually display the Fibonacci sequence. For example, students can use marbles or pennies.

8. Tell students that the final shot must have 144 of the chosen items.

9. Distribute copies of the 6–8 storyboard template (storyboard03.doc) and the shot list template (shotlist.doc). Give students time to work on their shot lists and storyboards in pairs. They will create these movies in pairs.

10. Then, students should research and gather as many ideas for their storyboards as possible. They'll be able to use images from clip art, scanned shots from magazines, digital cameras, video cameras, and the Internet. Encourage students to brainstorm many ideas for their projects.

11. Explain to students that this is the first step in the process of making their movies. They should continue to think and look for new everyday patterns. Remind the students that the more materials they have to work with, the more editing choices they will have. Remind them that it is better to have too many choices than not enough choices.

12. Give student pairs time to work on their projects.

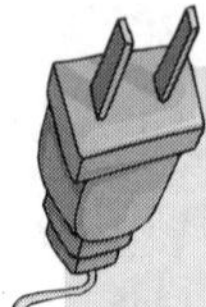

Extension Idea

Have students extend their Fibonacci numbers to the first 15 numbers (610 items).

Fibonacci Pattern Clips

Lesson Description

Students will capture and import still photographs and video footage that show Fibonacci sequences. Students will also learn to work with clips they have captured and imported by viewing, renaming, and adding clips to their movies.

Content Standard

Students will generalize from a pattern of observations made in particular cases, make conjectures, and provide supporting arguments for these conjectures.

Technology Skills

Students capture and import images, view and rename clips, and add clips to their movies.

Additional Technology Skill

- saving work

Materials

- digital camera
- video camera
- 6–8 patterns clips sample (pattern03_clip.avi; pattern03_clip.mov)

Teacher Preparation

1. Use the step-by-step directions included at the beginning of this book to teach students any necessary technology skills that they may not be familiar with.
2. Read the *Capturing and Importing Images* step-by-step directions (page 15; page015.pdf).
3. Read the *Working with Clips* step-by-step directions (page 16; page016.pdf).
4. A few days before this lesson, remind the students to continue gathering the materials for their Fibonacci sequences.

Procedure

1. Remind students about the previous lesson on Fibonacci numbers (*Fibonacci Patterns*). Have students partner up, and ask them to share the materials that they will be using to create their Fibonacci sequences.
2. Let student pairs demonstrate their ideas. Bring out the video camera, and have them tape each other for use in their movies.
3. Tell students that in this lesson they will learn how to capture and import still photographs and videos and then learn how to work with these clips. They will also learn how to view clips, rename them, and add clips to their movies.
4. Review the new technology skills of capturing and importing images and working with clips. Show the students the sample included on the CD (pattern03_clip.avi; pattern03_clip.mov).

Procedure *(cont.)*

5a. Model for students how to open their saved work. Start *Movie Maker*. Click **File** on the Menu bar. Click ***Open Project***. Go to the folder where your project is saved. Click the project you want to open. Click **Open**. Show a student's saved project.

5b. If using a Macintosh, start *iMovie*. Click **File**; click ***Open Project***. Go to the folder where your project is saved, click the project you want to open, and click **Open**.

6. Give student pairs time to capture and import their stills and videos.

7. Remind students that they will need at least 12 clips for their movies. Model the steps for students using the *Capturing and Importing Images* step-by-step directions (page 15; page015.pdf). Also, model the steps in the *Working with Clips* step-by-step directions (page 16; page016.pdf).

8. Clips will be saved in the Collections pane. Collections are libraries that contain the pictures that they have imported. They can use and reuse items from the collections for the movies they create. The Collections pane is found by clicking **File** on the Menu bar. (If using a Macintosh, clips will be saved in the Clips pane.)

9a. Model again for students how to view a clip. First, click **Collections** and choose the collection that contains the clip you want to watch. In the Contents pane, click the clip you want to watch. The clip appears on the Monitor pane. Click the **Play** button, and watch your clip.

9b. If using a Macintosh, click the **Clips** button to bring up the Clips pane. In the Clips pane, click the clip you want to watch. The clip appears in the Monitor window. Click the **Play** button to watch your clip. You can also drag the slider bar to move quickly through the clip.

10a. Model for students how to rename a clip. Right-click the clip you want to rename. Choose **Rename**. Type a new name for your clip.

10b. In Macintosh, double-click the clip you want to rename. Type a new name in the name field. Click **Set**, and your clip is renamed.

11. Show students how and where to save their work.

12. Remind students that this is an ongoing project and that they should continue to work on the Fibonacci sequences for their movies.

13. Review the rubric (page 157) with students so they understand how their work will be assessed. Give students time to work on their projects.

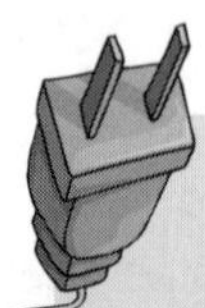

Extension Idea

Ask students to have someone videotape them for the opening of their movies before the next lesson. These videos should include the titles of their movies and introductions to their Fibonacci patterns.

Student Directions *Movie Maker*

Capturing and Importing Images

1. Click the **Start** menu.
2. Choose ***All Programs***.
3. Choose *Windows Movie Maker*.
4. If a new movie does not open, click **File** on the Menu bar. Click ***New Project***.
5. A new *Movie Maker* project opens.
6. To import an existing picture file, in the Movie Tasks pane, click ***Import Pictures***.
7. Go to the folder where your picture file is located.
8. Under Files of type, make sure *Picture Files* is selected.
9. Click the picture file you want.
10. Click **Import**.
11. The picture file imports. Now, it can be put into your movie.
12. The picture file appears in the Collections pane.
13. Save your work.

Student Directions *Movie Maker*

Working with Clips

1. To import a video from a camera, turn on the camera and connect it to the computer with a FireWire.
2. Set the camera to VTR mode. (Some cameras call this Play or VCR.)
3. In the Movie Tasks pane, click **Capture from the video device**.
4. Enter a filename for your file. Choose a place to save your file. Click **Next**.
5. Select ***Digital device format*** from the Video Setting. Click **Next**.
6. Select the Capture Method to capture parts of the tape manually. Click **Next**.
7. Use the DV camera controls to locate the beginning of the video you want to capture.
8. Select ***Start Capture*** to begin capturing the video.
9. Select ***Stop Capture*** to stop capturing the video.
10. Click **Finish** to close the Video Capture Wizard.
11. Your video clip is saved in the collection in the Contents pane.
12. Click the **Play** button to watch the clip. You can use the other Playback Controls to pause, stop, move forward or backward one frame at a time, fast forward, or rewind the clip.
13. To rename the clip, right-click the clip. Choose **Rename**. Type a new name for your clip.
14. Save your work.
15. Click, hold, and drag the clip down to the Timeline. As you move the clip over the Timeline, you will notice a vertical colored bar where it will be inserted if you let go of the mouse.
16. When the vertical colored bar is visible where you want your clip inserted, release the mouse button. The clip is added to your movie.

Assessment Rubric

Strong (3 points)	Students' work includes at least 12 video clips that show the Fibonacci sequence for the first 12 Fibonacci numbers.	Imported video clips contain focused content that support the project.	Students' work shows a strong understanding of the lesson objectives.
Effective (2 points)	Students' work includes 8–11 video clips that show the Fibonacci sequence for the first 12 Fibonacci numbers.	Imported video clips support the project.	Students' work shows an understanding of the lesson objectives.
Emerging (1 point)	Students' work includes 5–7 video clips that show the Fibonacci sequence for the first 12 Fibonacci numbers.	Imported video clips support the project. Some could be more focused.	Students' work shows an emerging understanding of the lesson objectives.
Not Yet (0 points)	Students' work includes 0–4 video clips that show the Fibonacci sequence for the first 12 Fibonacci numbers.	Imported video clips did not support the project.	Students' work shows a weak understanding of the lesson objectives.
Self Score			
Teacher Score			
Total Score			
Comment			

Fibonacci Sequences

Lesson Description

Students will learn to take the clips that they have already captured and imported and add them to Storyboard View or Clip Viewer.

Content Standard

Students will generalize from a pattern of observations made in particular cases, make conjectures, and provide supporting arguments for these conjectures.

Technology Skills

Students look at clips, arrange clips, and add or delete clips.

Additional Technology Skill

- saving work

Materials

- 6–8 patterns clips in order sample (pattern03_ordr.avi; pattern03_ordr.mov)

Teacher Preparation

1. Use the step-by-step directions included at the beginning of this book to teach students any necessary technology skills that they may not be familiar with.
2. Read the *Working in Storyboard View or Clip Viewer* step-by-step directions (page 17; page017.pdf).

Procedure

1. Remind students of the previous lessons about the Fibonacci sequence (*Fibonacci Patterns* and *Fibonacci Pattern Clips*). Today is a continuation of those lessons.
2. Give the students time to review their storyboards and shot lists. Let students take pictures or videos of any new sequences to add to their movies.
3. Then, ask a student to tell about his or her favorite movie. After he or she has shared, ask students if the movie would have made sense if the end had come at the beginning and the middle was at the end. Most students will probably say that the movie would not make sense in that order.
4. Remind students that events in movies are in a certain order to make sense. The movies they make need to be in order to make sense, too. Tell students that they will be organizing and arranging the clips that they have already captured and imported with Storyboard View or Clip Viewer.
5. Show students the sample patterns clips provided on the CD (pattern03_ordr.avi; pattern03_ordr.mov).

Procedure *(cont.)*

6. Explain that Storyboard View or Clip Viewer is the next step in the process of making their movies. Storyboard View or Clip Viewer shows the sequence of the clips in their movies.

7. Explain to students that with this technology they will be able to put their clips in order, delete any clips that are not working for them, add any new clips they have, and arrange them in order for their movies.

8a. Model for students how to open their saved work. Start *Movie Maker*. Click **File** on the Menu bar. Click ***Open Project***. Go to the folder where your project is saved. Click the project you want to open. Click **Open**. Show a student's saved project.

8b. If using a Macintosh, start *iMovie*. Click **File**; click ***Open Project***. Go to the folder where your project is saved, click the project you want to open, and click **Open**.

9. Let students work with their partners to add any new clips or images to their movies and edit their movies using Storyboard View or Clip Viewer.

10. Remind students to save their work.

11. Review the rubric (page 161) with students so they understand how their work will be assessed.

Extension Idea

Have students create additional mathematical sequences of their choice. Post these sequences on the board, and see if other students can solve the sequences. Students can add clips or images of the new sequences and compare them to the Fibonacci sequence.

Student Directions *Movie Maker*

1. To arrange clips, locate the clip you want to move.
2. Click, hold, and drag the desired clip along the storyboard. As you move the clip along the storyboard, you will notice a vertical colored bar where the clip will be relocated if you release the mouse button.
3. When the vertical colored bar is visible where you want your clip to be moved, release the mouse button. The clip will move to that position.
4. Find a new clip you want to add into your movie. These clips should be in your Collections pane.
5. Click, hold, and drag the clip down to the storyboard. As you move the clip over the storyboard, you will notice a vertical colored bar where the clip will be inserted if you release the mouse button.
6. When the vertical colored bar is visible where you want your clip inserted, release the mouse button. The clip will be added to your movie.
7. To delete a clip, find the clip you want to delete.
8. Right-click the clip.
9. Choose **Delete** from the pop-up menu.
10. The clip is deleted from your movie.
11. Save your work.

Assessment Rubric

Strong (3 points)	Students were creative in arranging the sequence in Storyboard View or Clip Viewer by experimenting with adding, deleting, and rearranging photographs and videos.	Students' work shows a strong understanding of the lesson objectives.
Effective (2 points)	Students experimented in Storyboard View or Clip Viewer by adding and rearranging photographs and videos.	Students' work shows an understanding of the lesson objectives.
Emerging (1 point)	Students experimented with Storyboard View or Clip Viewer by rearranging photographs and videos.	Students' work shows an emerging understanding of the lesson objectives.
Not Yet (0 points)	Students did not experiment with Storyboard View or Clip Viewer.	Students' work shows a weak understanding of the lesson objectives.
Self Score		
Teacher Score		
Total Score		
Comments		

Giving Titles to Fibonacci Sequences

Lesson Description
Students will learn how to add titles and credits to their movies. Students will also learn how to change the colors, fonts, styles, and sizes of their titles.

Content Standard
Students will generalize from a pattern of observations made in particular cases, make conjectures, and provide supporting arguments for these conjectures

Technology Skills
Students add titles to the beginnings of their movies and credits to the ends of their movies. Students change the colors, fonts, styles, and sizes of their titles.

Additional Technology Skills
- saving work
- capturing and importing images
- using Storyboard View or Clip Viewer

Materials
- 6–8 patterns movie sample with titles and credits (pattern03_crdts.avi; pattern03_crdts.mov)

Teacher Preparation

1. Use the step-by-step directions included at the beginning of this book to teach students any necessary technology skills that they may not be familiar with.
2. Read the *Adding Titles and Credits* step-by-step directions (page 18; page018.pdf).

Procedure

1. Remind students of the previous lessons about the Fibonacci sequence (*Fibonacci Patterns, Fibonacci Pattern Clips*, and *Fibonacci Sequences*). Today is a continuation of those lessons.
2. Have each student write his or her favorite movie or book title on the board. Discuss why they like these titles. Then, discuss some of their favorite movies or books to get them thinking about titles.
3. Write the word *money* on the board. Brainstorm with the class some titles that they think would work for a movie about money. You could suggest *Money Hungry*. Once they come up with these titles, explain that they will be creating titles for their movies. They will have to think creatively to come up with original titles for their Fibonacci Patterns movies.

Procedure *(cont.)*

4. Tell students that the text they add anywhere in their movies could be titles. Titles can be added at the beginning, the end, over an existing clip, and before or after a clip. For this lesson, they will learn how to add titles at the beginnings and ends of their movies. The titles at the end of the movies are called *credits*. The credits tell about the people involved in making the movie.

5. Show students the sample movie provided on the CD (pattern03_crdts.avi; pattern03_crdts.mov).

6. Have students work with their partners to come up with creative, fun, and interesting titles for their movies.

7. Explain to the students that they will be adding titles to their movies (at the beginning and on each page) and adding credits at the ends of their movies. Explain that they will also have opportunities to change the colors, fonts, styles, and sizes of their titles.

8. Review the technology skill to be used—adding titles. Adding a title at the beginning is a good way to display the movie title. Students will also need to add titles to each page. Credits at the end are titles that conclude their movies. Changing the color, font, style, and size is a good way to be creative with titles.

9. Give the student pairs time to open their projects, review their projects, and capture and import any new clips.

10. Remind students to save their finished work.

11. Review the rubric (page 165) with students so that they understand how their work will be assessed.

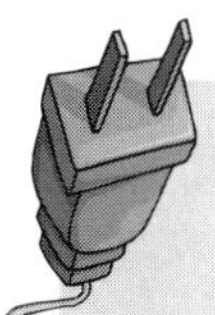

Extension Idea

Have students experiment with animating titles. Students can zoom into titles and then zoom out. Students can make the titles come in from the left side, move across the screen, and exit on the right side.

Student Directions *Movie Maker*

1. To add a title to the beginning of your movie, click the **Show Storyboard** button to display the storyboard.
2. Select **Tools** on the Menu bar. Click ***Titles and Credits...***. Choose *Add titles at the beginning of the movie*.
3. Type what you would like to include on the slide.
4. Click *Done, add title to movie*. Your title clip is added to the beginning of the movie.
5. Click the **Play** button to preview the title in the Monitor pane.
6. To add credits, click **Tools** on the Menu bar. Select ***Titles and Credits...***. Choose *Add credits at the end of the movie*.
7. Type the closing text (for example, *Produced by: [your name and your partner's name]*).
8. Click *Done, add title to movie*. Your ending credits are added to the end of the movie.
9. Click the **Play** button to preview the title in the Monitor pane.
10. To change the style, color, or font, right-click the title or credits clip and choose **Edit Title...** from the pop-up menu.
11. In the Enter Text for Title pane, click *Change the text font and color*.
12. In the Select Title Font and Color pane, choose a different font from the Font drop-down menu.
13. Choose a style and color for your text. To increase or decrease text size, click *Size options*.
14. Choose a position or justification for your text. You can align the text on the left, in the center, or on the right.
15. When the text attributes are set to your satisfaction, click **Done** to apply them to the titles or credits.
16. Save your work.

Assessment Rubric

Strong (3 points)	Movie includes an opening title, title on each page, and closing credits, that accurately describe the movie.	Creative use of fonts, styles, colors, and sizes create visually appealing titles and closing credits.	Students' work shows a strong understanding of the lesson objectives.
Effective (2 points)	Movie includes an opening title and closing credits but not a title on each page.	Students were able to use font, style, color, and size applications in either the title or credits but not both.	Students' work shows an understanding of the lesson objectives.
Emerging (1 point)	Movie includes either an opening title or closing credits, but not both.	Students used one of the applications: font, style, color, or size.	Students' work shows an emerging understanding of the lesson objectives.
Not Yet (0 points)	Movie does not include titles or credits.	Students did not use font, style, color, or size applications.	Students' work shows a weak understanding of the lesson objectives.
Self Score			
Teacher Score			
Total Score			
Comments			

Fibonacci Patterns Movie

Lesson Description

Students will use AutoMovie or Magic iMovie to complete their movies.

Content Standard

Students will generalize from a pattern of observations made in particular cases, make conjectures, and provide supporting arguments for these conjectures.

Technology Skill

Students pick styles and transitions for their movies.

Additional Technology Skills

- using Storyboard View or Clip Viewer
- saving work

Materials

- 6–8 patterns movie sample (pattern03_movie.avi; pattern03_movie.mov)

Teacher Preparation

1. Use the step-by-step directions included at the beginning of this book to teach students any necessary technology skills that they may not be familiar with.
2. Read the *Using AutoMovie or Magic iMovie* step-by-step directions (page 19; page019.pdf).
3. Let the students know that they will be finishing their movies. Explain to them that this will be their last opportunity to add any new materials to their projects.

Procedure

1. Remind students of the previous lessons about the Fibonacci sequence (*Fibonacci Patterns*, *Fibonacci Pattern Clips*, *Fibonacci Sequences*, and *Giving Titles to Fibonacci Sequences*). Today is the culmination of those lessons. Explain to the students that they will be finishing their movies today with the technology called AutoMovie or Magic iMovie.
2. Go over how to use AutoMovie or Magic iMovie. Explain that AutoMovie or Magic iMovie is a shortcut for them in producing their movies. AutoMovie or Magic iMovie will build and edit their movies based on the clips and titles they have stored in Storyboard View or Clip Viewer.

3a. Model for students how to open their saved work. Start *Movie Maker*. Click **File** on the Menu bar. Click ***Open Project***. Go to the folder where your project is saved. Click the project you want to open. Click **Open**. Show a student's saved project.

Procedure *(cont.)*

3b. If using a Macintosh, start *iMovie*. Click **File**; click ***Open Project***. Go to the folder where your project is saved, click the project you want to open, and click **Open**.

4. Give students time to review their saved work and to capture and import any new photographs. Have students share any new pattern videos they have found.

5. Review how to add titles and credits and how to change colors, fonts, styles, and sizes.

6. Show students the sample patterns movie provided on the CD (pattern03_movie.avi; pattern03_movie.mov).

7. Have students review their movies two or three times to see if there are any changes to be made to the colors, fonts, sizes, or styles of the type. Students should make at least one change to their movies.

8. Remind students to save their work.

9. When students have completed their movies, allow them to play their movies for the class.

10. Review the rubric (page 169) with students so they understand how their work will be assessed.

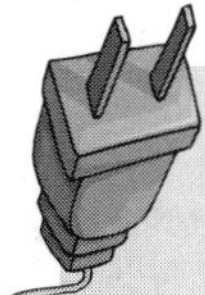

Extension Idea

Instead of using AutoMovie or Magic iMovie, have the students edit their movies themselves using available technology.

Student Directions *Movie Maker*

1. Click **Tools** on the Menu bar.
2. Click ***AutoMovie...***.
3. The AutoMovie wizard appears.
4. Click a ***Highlights Movie*** style.
5. Click *Done, edit movie.*
6. All your transitions and titles are added to the Storyboard.
7. Make sure the Playhead is at the beginning of the movie.
8. Click the Monitors pane **Play** button to play the AutoMovie.
9. Save your work.

Assessment Rubric

Strong (3 points)	Movie shows at least 12 clips or pictures that show patterns.	Movie is visually appealing, and the titles improve the presentation.	Students completed the work independently.	Students' work shows a strong understanding of the lesson objectives.
Effective (2 points)	Movie shows 8–11 clips or pictures.	Movie is visually appealing and titles are used.	Students completed the work with some support.	Students' work shows an understanding of the lesson objectives.
Emerging (1 point)	Movie shows 5–7 clips or pictures.	Movie is somewhat visually appealing.	Students completed the work with a lot of support.	Students' work shows an emerging understanding of the lesson objectives.
Not Yet (0 points)	Movie shows 0–4 clips or pictures.	Movie is visually unappealing, and no titles were used.	Students did not complete the work.	Students' work shows a weak understanding of the lesson objectives.
Self Score				
Teacher Score				
Total Score				
Comments				

Historical Figures

Lesson Description

Student will learn how to add a title before and after a clip that they have already captured and imported in Storyboard View or Clip Viewer.

Content Standard

Students will understand that specific individuals and the values those individuals held had an impact on history.

Technology Skill

Students add titles before and after clips.

Additional Technology skills

- capturing and importing still images and videos
- using Storyboard View or Clip Viewer
- saving work

Materials

- digital camera
- video camera
- 6–8 storyboard template (storyboard03.doc)
- shot list template (shotlist.doc)
- pictures or videos from home, newspapers, magazines, clip art, and the Internet of historical figures

Teacher Preparation

1. It is recommended that the Social Studies lessons (pages 170–189) be taught as a unit so that students create completed movies. Use the step-by-step directions included at the beginning of this book to teach students any necessary technology skills that they may not be familiar with.

2. Read the *Adding Titles Before and After a Clip* step-by-step directions (page 20; page020.pdf).

3. Bring in books about historical individuals from the library. Bookmark Internet sites that are appropriate for students to perform further research.

4. Put the following names on the blackboard: *Indira Ghandi*, *Abraham Lincoln*, *Clara Barton*, *Rosa Parks*, *Martin Luther King Jr.*, *Jimmy Carter*, *Mother Theresa*, and *Sally Ride*. Ask these questions: *Who are these people? Why are they famous? What types of values did they have that made them famous?*

5. Explain to students that they will be making movies about people whom they admire and who had an impact on history. The choices are endless. Challenge students to think hard about whom these people might be. Tell students that they should begin their research and decide whom they will feature in their movies, before the next class. Tell students to start gathering materials for their movies and bring them to the next class.

Procedure

1. Ask students to give brief descriptions of the people they are basing their movies on. Rather than just telling their classmates whom they want to feature, have students give some clues so the class can guess whom they are describing.

2. Explain to students that while we know, for example, that Jimmy Carter was the 39th president of the United States, he is also known for working for peace and human rights. He won the Nobel Peace Prize in 2002 and gives his time and effort working for Habitat for Humanity. These are some of the values that make him a great leader.

3. Tell students that they will be making movies about historical figures. For these movies, each student will need at least 12 video clips or stills that show how their chosen individual has made an impact on history.

4. Give students time to continue their research and gather images and video clips.

5. Distribute copies of the 6–8 storyboard template (storyboard03.doc) and the shot list template (shotlist.doc). Give the students time to work on their storyboards and shot lists. Remind them that their storyboard details the ideas for their video projects, including any stills, video, text, and music. Remind them that they will need to keep their storyboards up-to-date.

6. Explain to students that in this lesson they are going to learn how to add a title before and after clips. Explain that adding a title before a new scene is a good way to introduce it. Adding a title after a scene is a good way to review it.

7. Have students capture and import stills and videos as listed in their storyboards.

8. Remind students how to save their work.

9. Tell students that they should continue to research their chosen individual. Remind them that the more material they have to work with, the more editing choices they will have. It is better to have too many choices than not enough.

10. Review the rubric (page 173) so that students understand how their work will be assessed.

Extension Idea

Have students complete similar movies based on a teacher, a coach, or a mentor that has had an impact on their lives.

Student Directions *Movie Maker*

1. Click **Show Storyboard**.
2. Select the clip that you want your title to come before or after.
3. Click **Tools** on the Menu bar.
4. Click ***Titles and Credits...***.
5. Click *Add title before the selected clip* or *Add title after the selected clip*.
6. Type primary text.
7. Type secondary text.
8. Click *Change the text font and color*. Choose a font and the color that you want the font to be. You can be very creative with this.
9. Click *Change the title animation*. This is where you get to decide how you want the title to appear. It can fly in, fade in and out, or just appear.
10. Select *Done, add title to movie*.
11. Your title clip is added.
12. Click the **Play** button to preview the title in the Monitor pane.

Assessment Rubric

Strong (3 points)	Work includes at least 12 photographs or video clips depicting a historical figure.	Storyboard is complete and shows great detail. Titles are pertinent to the concept.	Student's work shows a strong understanding of the lesson objectives.
Effective (2 points)	Work includes 9–11 photographs or video clips depicting a historical figure.	Storyboard is complete but could include more detail. Title is chosen for the movie, but few others are used throughout.	Student's work shows an understanding of the lesson objectives.
Emerging (1 point)	Work includes 6–8 photographs or video clips depicting a historical figure.	Storyboard is complete but includes little detail. Title is chosen for the movie. No additional titles were chosen.	Student's work shows an emerging understanding of the lesson objectives.
Not Yet (0 points)	Work includes 1–5 photographs or video clips depicting a historical figure.	Storyboard is incomplete, showing no detail. No titles were chosen for the movie.	Student's work shows a weak understanding of the lesson objectives.
Self Score			
Teacher Score			
Total Score			
Comments			

Historical Figures on a Timeline

Lesson Description

Students will learn how to work with audio tracks that they have recorded with a video camera. Students will learn how to use Timeline View or Timeline Viewer.

Content Standard

Students will understand that specific individuals and the values those individuals held had impacts on history.

Technology Skill

Students work with audio tracks recorded with a video camera.

Additional Technology Skills

- capturing and importing still images and videos
- using Storyboard View or Clip Viewer
- working with titles
- saving work

Materials

- digital camera
- video camera

Teacher Preparation

1. Use the step-by-step directions included at the beginning of this book to teach students any necessary technology skills that they may not be familiar with.
2. Read the *Working with Audio* step-by-step directions (pages 21–22; page021.pdf). These directions include how to import an audio file and how to work with Timeline View or Timeline View(er).
3. Record at least two sample videos with audio so that students can see what is expected. One sample should be clear and set in a quiet background. The other sample should be taped in a noisy area so students can see how noise interferes with the audio.

Procedure

1. Remind students of the previous lesson about historical figures (*Historical Figures*). This lesson is a continuation of that lesson.
2. Share the sample video clips with the class. Ask if the video clips are clear. Ask if the students can understand what is being said. Can they hear any background noise that interferes with their enjoyment of the video? Do they think including audio would help or hurt their movies?

Procedure *(cont.)*

3. Explain to students that this lesson covers how to work with audio tracks. Tell them that they will be using video cameras to record someone talking about the historical figures chosen. Students can tape themselves, find someone in the school who is willing to be taped, or tape people at home. The taping can be done in whatever style the student chooses—maybe in interview fashion or just a recital of the facts. Many video cameras today have built-in microphones. Explain to the students that when they record audio, they should be very careful and aware of background noise. They should try to record the audio in a quiet place.

4. Give students time to shoot at least three video clips so they can have choices for editing. Have students experiment with different camera angles—long shots, medium shots, and close-up shots. After taping, students can decide which audio clip(s) should be included in their movies. Tell them they can include more than one audio clip if they feel that it works.

5. Explain to students that in this lesson they will work with audio tracks using Timeline View or Timeline Viewer. Model for students how to use Timeline View(er) to import and work with audio clips.

6. Remind that while Timeline View(er) is very similar to Storyboard View or Clip Viewer, it is more concerned with time and less with sequence.

7. Give students time to capture and import any new videos or still images they have.

8. Have students update their storyboards to include any new images or titles. Remind them that keeping their storyboards and shot lists current will help them be organized. Remind them that they should include their new video clips in their storyboards.

9. Review the rubric (page 177) with students so that they understand how their work will be assessed.

10. Tell students that in their next lesson they will learn how to work with music. Ask them to bring in at least four pieces of music they think will be great additions to their movies. Have them try different styles of music—jazz, hip hop, period pieces, or classical.

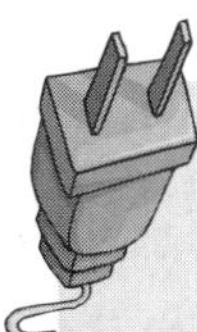

Extension Ideas

Have students experiment with sound effects by designing a sound effects track for their movies. This track could be in place of music or in addition to it. By adding this additional layer, students will have to be careful to balance out the effects with the music so that everything can be heard.

Student Directions *Movie Maker*

1. In the Collections pane, select the collection where you want the audio file stored.
2. Click **File** on the Menu bar.
3. Click ***Import into Collections***.
4. Choose the folder that contains the audio file you want to import. Select the audio file.
5. Click **Import**.
6. The audio file is added to the collection you chose in step 1.
7. Drag the audio clip to the desired location in the Audio or Music track in the Timeline.
8. The audio clip is added to your movie.
9. Click the **Set Audio Levels** button in the Timeline.
10. Drag the slider to adjust the audio balance. Dragging it to the right will increase the Audio or Music volume level while decreasing the audio from the video volume level. Dragging it to the left will do the opposite.
11. When you are done, click the **X** in the upper right-hand corner of the box to close the Audio Levels dialog box.

Words to Know in Timeline View

- **Video track**—This is the track that holds all the video clips in your movie. Any sound that is associated with the video will be on the Audio track. The Video track also holds Titles and Credits clips if they were added before or after a clip.
- **Transition track**—This track holds any transitions you have added to your movie. You will be working with transitions in a later lesson.
- **Audio track**—The audio clips on this track are automatically placed here when you import video that contains audio.
- **Audio/Music track**—This track contains your music track.
- **Title Overlay track**—This track holds titles and credits.
- **Playback Controls**—You can use these controls to play, pause, and rewind your movie.

Assessment Rubric

Strong (3 points)	Student videotaped at least three clips.	Video clips support the content of the movie. Audio is clear with no background noises.	Student successfully imported the video clips and experimented with editing choices.	Student's work shows a strong understanding of the lesson objectives.
Effective (2 points)	Student videotaped two clips.	Video clips support the content of the movie. The audio is clear, but there are some background noises.	Student successfully imported the video clips.	Student's work shows an understanding of the lesson objectives.
Emerging (1 point)	Student videotaped one clip.	Video clip supports the content of the movie. The sound is interrupted by background noise.	Student successfully imported a video clip, but needed assistance.	Student's work shows an emerging understanding of the lesson objectives.
Not Yet (0 points)	Student did not videotape any clips.	Student had no clips to include in his or her movie.	Student was unable to import video clips.	Student's work shows a weak understanding of the lesson objectives.
Self Score				
Teacher Score				
Total Score				
Comments				

Making Music Work

Lesson Description

Students will learn how to work with music tracks.

Content Standard

Students will understand that specific individuals and the values those individuals held had an impact on history.

Technology Skill

Students work with music tracks and add them to their movies.

Additional Technology Skills

- saving work
- capturing and importing video or audio
- using Storyboard View or Clip Viewer
- using Timeline View or Timeline Viewer

Materials

- digital camera
- video camera
- CDs, cassettes, or iTunes song lists containing their music choices

Teacher Preparation

1. Use the step-by-step directions included at the beginning of this book to teach students any necessary technology skills that they may not be familiar with.
2. Read the *Working with Music* step-by-step directions (page 23; page023.pdf).
3. Remind students that in the previous lesson they were asked to research at least four music choices for their movies. Have them bring these choices to school.

Procedure

1. Remind students of the previous lessons about historical figures (*Historical Figures* and *Historical Figures on a Timeline*). This lesson is a continuation of those lessons.
2. Ask students if they have any new photographs or videos they would like to add to their projects, and have them share these with the class.
3. Divide the class into groups and have students share their music tracks with their groups. With their classmates' help, have each student choose a track for his or her movie.
4. Explain to students that in this lesson they will learn how to work with music tracks and add them to their movies.

Procedure *(cont.)*

5. Demonstrate working with audio. In the Movie Tasks pane, click **Import audio or music**. Go to the folder where your audio file is located. Under Files of type, make sure ***Audio and Music files*** is selected. Click the desired audio file. Click **Import**. Then, the audio file will import and appear in the Contents pane.
6. Ask students these questions: *Does the music track support and enhance their story? Does it move the story along? Is it too quick or too slow? Does it distract or add to the overall production?*
7. Model for students how to use Timeline View(er) to import their music.
8. Have students import all of the music tracks they have selected. Having more options will help in the editing phase. However, have each of them only place one chosen song in the actual movie file. The rest can stay in the Audio pane.
9. Remind students to save their work.
10. Give the students time to work on their projects.
11. Review the rubric (page 181) so that students understand how their work will be assessed.

Extension Ideas

Have students find other ways to gather music for their movies. They can record themselves playing musical instruments, or they could record the school band or chorus.

Student Directions *Movie Maker*

If importing an audio file from a CD:

1. Place the audio CD into your computer's CD or DVD drive.
2. Click the **Audio** button to bring up the Audio pane.
3. The CD title will show in the pull-down menu.
4. Locate the song you want to import into your movie.
5. Drag the song from the Audio pane to the desired position on the Timeline.
6. The CD audio will be inserted in the Timeline.

If importing an audio file from iTunes:

1. Click the **Audio** button. This will open the Audio pane.
2. Your iTunes library is listed in the Audio pane.
3. Your teacher can help you click the pop-up menu. Choose your iTunes playlist.
4. If you cannot find the song, type a word or phrase in the Search field. The computer will look for the song.
5. Click on the song that you want. Hold your mouse button down. Drag the song from the Audio pane to where you want it on the Timeline.
6. The audio file from iTunes will be inserted in the Timeline.

Assessment Rubric

Strong (3 points)	Student experimented with at least four different music tracks.	Music tracks enhance and support the content of the movie. Music is creative and interesting.	Student's work shows a strong understanding of the lesson objectives.
Effective (2 points)	Student experimented with three different music tracks.	Music tracks support the content of the movie.	Student's work shows an understanding of the lesson objectives.
Emerging (1 point)	Student experimented with two different music tracks.	Music tracks support the content of the movie, but the music could be more interesting.	Student's work shows an emerging understanding of the lesson objectives.
Not Yet (0 points)	Student experimented with one music track.	Student's music does not support the content of the movie, and at times it is distracting.	Student's work shows a weak understanding of the lesson objectives.
Self Score			
Teacher Score			
Total Score			
Comments			

Sequencing the Movie

Lesson Description

Students will learn how to work further with the clips they have chosen for their movies. Students will learn how to rearrange clip sequences and delete clips from their movies.

Content Standard

Students will understand that specific individuals and the values those individuals held had impacts on history.

Technology Skill

Students rearrange clips and delete clips from their movies.

Additional Technology Skills

- saving work
- capturing and importing video
- using Storyboard View or Clip Viewer
- using Timeline View or Timeline Viewer

Materials

- digital camera
- video camera
- two video samples (video A is a completed sample; video B is the same as A, but its frames are out of order)

Teacher Preparation

1. Use the step-by-step directions included at the beginning of this book to teach students any necessary technology skills that they may not be familiar with.

2. Read the *Rearranging Clip Sequences and Deleting Clips* step-by-step directions (page 24; page024.pdf).

3. Read the step-by-step directions from *Working with Clips* (page 16; page016.pdf).

4. If possible, prepare an example of a movie that has already been completed. Then, rearrange the sequence to demonstrate another choice. These sequences are called *video A* and *video B* in the procedure section.

Procedure

1. Remind students of the previous lessons about historical figures (*Historical Figures, Historical Figures on a Timeline,* and *Making Music Work*). This lesson is a continuation of those lessons.

2. Play a completed movie (video A) for students. Then, play the same movie again with a different sequence of shots (video B). Ask students which video works better, A or B. Why? Does changing the order of the shots help or hurt the message? Does the video become too choppy?

Procedure *(cont.)*

3. Explain to students that in this lesson they are going to learn how to work with the clips they have already captured and imported into their movies. They will learn how to take these clips, change the order, and delete some if necessary.

4. Model for students how to rearrange and delete clips. You can rearrange or delete clips while in Timeline View(er) or Storyboard View (Clip Viewer).

5. Work with students to create different sequences of their movies by rearranging and deleting clips. Have them try at least three versions. Give them time to work on this process. Then, have students decide which version works best.

6. Tell students that in the next lesson they will be finishing their movies. Tell them to review their movies before the next lesson to make sure they are happy with them. They will need to make any necessary changes before the next lesson. Ask students if they have any new photographs, videos, or music tracks they would like to add to their projects. Tell students that this will be their last chance to add any new material.

7. Give students time to capture and import any new materials.

8. Have students update their storyboards to include any new images or titles.

9. Remind students to save their work.

10. Review the rubric (page 185) with students so that they understand how their work will be assessed.

Extension Idea

Have students complete similar movies about what their historical figure would be doing in the world today. Would that figure be fighting in a war? Running for president? Building schools in foreign countries? Fighting hunger? Helping the sick?

Student Directions *Movie Maker*

Rearranging Clip Sequences

1. Find the clip you want to rearrange.
2. Click on the clip. Hold your mouse button down. Drag the clip along the Timeline. As you move the clip along the Timeline, you will see a vertical colored bar where it will be rearranged if you let go of the mouse.
3. When the vertical colored bar is where you want your clip rearranged, release the mouse button and the clip is rearranged to that position.

Deleting a Clip from Your Movie

1. Find the clip you want to delete.
2. Right-click on the clip.
3. Choose **Delete** from the pop-up menu.
4. The clip is deleted from your movie.

Assessment Rubric

Strong (3 points)	Student experimented with at least three different sequences.	Final sequence is strong and is visually appealing. All clips strongly support the project.	Student completed the work independently.	Student's work shows a strong understanding of the lesson objectives.
Effective (2 points)	Student experimented with at least two different sequences.	Final sequence is visually appealing. All clips are pertinent to the project.	Student completed the work with a little support.	Student's work shows an understanding of the lesson objectives.
Emerging (1 point)	Student experimented with at least one sequence.	Final sequence works. However, some of the clips are not pertinent and should have been edited.	Student completed the work with some support.	Student's work shows an emerging understanding of the lesson objectives.
Not Yet (0 points)	Student experimented with a sequence by just deleting or adding a scene.	Final sequence is visually unappealing.	Student completed the work with a lot of support, or work was not completed.	Student's work shows a weak understanding of the lesson objectives.
Self Score				
Teacher Score				
Total Score				
Comments				

Historical Figures—The Video

Lesson Description

Students will experiment with different AutoMovie or Magic iMovie styles and transitions to complete their movies.

Content Standard

Students will understand that specific individuals and the values those individuals held had impacts on history.

Technology Skill

Students use different styles or transitions to complete their movies.

Additional Technology Skills

- using Timeline View or Timeline Viewer
- saving work

Teacher Preparation

1. Use the step-by-step directions included at the beginning of this book to teach students any necessary technology skills that they may not be familiar with.

2. Read the *Using AutoMovie or Magic iMovie* step-by-step directions (page 19; page019.pdf)

3. Read the *Selecting a Movie Style* step-by-step directions (page 25; page025.pdf).

Procedure

1. Remind students of the previous lessons about historical figures (*Historical Figures*, *Historical Figures on a Timeline*, *Making Music Work*, and *Sequencing the Movie*). This lesson is the culmination of those lessons.

2. Get the students excited by letting them know that they will be finishing their movies. Explain that this will be the last opportunity for them to make any changes.

3. Remind students that they have already used this technology. Now they will be taking it a step further in this lesson by experimenting with different transitions or styles. A *transition* is the way one scene blends into another.

4. Go over how to use AutoMovie or Magic iMovie. Discuss different styles and transitions that are available in the programs.

Procedure *(cont.)*

5. Have students open their saved work and review it. Ask these questions: *Does the movie represent their chosen individual and the values that individual held that impacted history?*

6. Remind students to look at the scenes, the music, the titles (font, color, and style), and the sequence of their movies to see if there is any room for improvement.

7. Give students time to make any changes and select styles for their movies. Have them experiment with different styles to see which one works best. Explain to the students why one style might work better than others. (In AutoMovie, if the music track is slow, a Highlights Movie might work best. If the music track has a fast pace, perhaps the Music Video style will work best.)

8. Model for students how to review their AutoMovie. Make sure the Playhead is at the beginning of the movie. Click the **Play** button on the Monitor pane to play the movie.

9. Remind students to save their work.

10. When students have completed the reviews of their movies, allow students to play their movies for the class.

11. Review the rubric (page 189) so that students understand how their work will be assessed.

Extension Idea

Have students create similar movies using titles only. Designing titles along with sound effects and music can be an interesting way to portray their historical figures.

Student Directions *Movie Maker*

1. Click **Tools** on the Menu bar.
2. Click ***AutoMovie...***.
3. The AutoMovie wizard appears.
4. Select an AutoMovie editing style (see below).
5. Click *Done, edit movie.*

Types of Styles in AutoMovie

- **Highlights Movie**—This movie style has fast and slow transitions between clips. There is a title at the beginning of the movie. There are credits at the end of the movie.
- **Music Video**—This style matches the music. There are quick edits for a fast pace, and long edits for slower clips. The speed of the style is based on the music's beat.
- **Sports Highlights**—This style adds excitement to the movie.

Assessment Rubric

Strong (3 points)	Commercial idea completely explains the concept.	Storyboard includes great detail.	Student's work shows a strong understanding of the lesson objectives.
Effective (2 points)	Commercial idea explains the concept.	Storyboard includes details.	Student's work shows an understanding of the lesson objectives.
Emerging (1 point)	Commercial idea somewhat explains the concept.	Storyboard is somewhat detailed.	Student's work shows an emerging understanding of the lesson objectives.
Not Yet (0 points)	Commercial idea does not explain the concept.	Storyboard is incomplete and shows very little detail.	Student's work shows a weak understanding of the lesson objectives.
Self Score			
Teacher Score			
Total Score			

Comments

Assessment Rubric

Strong (3 points)	Movie shows at least 12 photographs and/or video clips.	Movie is visually appealing, and the titles improve the presentation.	Transitions enhance the content of the movie.	Student's work shows a strong understanding of the lesson objectives.
Effective (2 points)	Movie shows 9–11 photographs and/or video clips.	Movie is visually appealing, and titles were used.	Transitions somewhat enhance the content of the movie.	Student's work shows an understanding of the lesson objectives.
Emerging (1 point)	Movie shows 6–8 photographs and/or video clips.	Movie is somewhat visually appealing.	Some of the transitions enhance the content of the movie, while a few of them detract from it.	Student's work shows an emerging understanding of the lesson objectives.
Not Yet (0 points)	Movie shows at least five photographs and/or movie clips.	Movie is visually unappealing, and no titles were used.	Transitions detract from the overall flow of the movie.	Student's work shows a weak understanding of the lesson objectives.
Self Score				
Teacher Score				
Total Score				

Comments

The Ecosystem—HELP!

Lesson Description

Students will learn how various techniques, such as camera positions, camera angles, and sound quality, can help them make excellent movies. For this lesson, they will use these skills and begin making television commercials.

Content Standard

Students will know factors that affect the number and types of organisms an ecosystem can support (e.g., available resources, disease, competition from other organisms, predation).

Technology Skill

Students learn various techniques such as camera position and sound quality.

Additional Technology Skills

- saving work
- capturing and importing

Materials

- 6–8 storyboard template (storyboard03.doc)
- copies of *Filming Techniques* (page 26; page026.pdf)

Teacher Preparation

1. It is recommended that the Science lessons (pages 190–208) be taught as a unit so that students create completed movies. Use the step-by-step directions included at the beginning of this book to teach students any necessary technology skills that they may not be familiar with.
2. Gather at least three TV commercials to review with the class. Record these at home, or download them from Internet sites. If possible, find different styles for each commercial. Some examples include fast-paced or action commercials, talking-head commercials (one person speaking to camera), or simple commercials with titles only. Animated commercials or commercials with special effects should not be used at this time.

Procedure

1. Explain to students that television commercials are used to market products or ideas. Then play for students the three commercials. Ask the following questions: *What was the message or product in each commercial? Are these memorable commercials? Was there music? Were there titles? Were there logos or taglines?* Point out to students that there are many different types of commercials. Two elements that make a good commercial are a clear message and entertainment value.
2. Write these phrases on the board—*shopping with your friends*, *shopping at the supermarket*, *planting trees*, *riding your bicycle*, and *birthday party*.

Procedure *(cont.)*

3. Tell students that they will be making television commercials about simple things that they can do in their everyday lives to benefit the ecosystem. The commercial should be 30 seconds long.
4. Review the phrases on the board. Ask the class to think about what these phrases have to do with the ecosystem. Brainstorm with the class some possible ideas for their commercials, using the phrases on the board as topics. An idea for a commercial titled "Parties" could be the following scenario: We see a party taking place and notice that there are no paper plates, napkins, or plastic anywhere. The packages we see are wrapped in brown paper, and the ribbon and cards are all reused from previous gifts. For gifts, we see a shot of the "gift of giving", like babysitting or lawn mowing, instead of material gifts.
5. Distribute copies of the 6–8 storyboard template (storyboard03.doc). and copies of *Filming Techniques* (page 26).
6. As an exercise, have students again review the commercials you brought. They should each pick one and do a storyboard for that commercial. Have them examine what types of shots are in the commercial (close-up shots, wide shots, long shots, pans, or zooms). They should make note of these on their storyboards. Other things to describe in the storyboards are actors, props, different locations, notes on dialog, and voice-over narration. Remind them to add titles to their storyboard frames when titles are used.
7. Remind students that when there is music throughout the commercial, they should indicate this at the beginning of their storyboards using the words *music throughout*.
8. Now have students review their storyboards by comparing them to the finished commercial examples.
9. Have students start to work on their storyboards for their own commercials. Explain that they will be working on this commercial for a few lessons so their storyboards will be continually updated as they gather more materials.
10. Tell students to continue to work on their projects by keeping in mind how to shoot the different camera angles, movements, and shots.
11. Review the rubric (page 192) so that students will see how their work will be assessed.

Extension Idea

Sometimes using still photographs and titles are very powerful. Have the students create commercials using only still photographs, titles, and music to tell their stories.

The Ecosystem in 30 Seconds

Lesson Description
Students will learn how to use video effects in their commercials.

Content Standard
Students will know factors that affect the number and types of organisms an ecosystem can support (e.g., available resources; disease; competition from other organisms; predation).

Technology Skill
Students use video effects in movies.

Additional Technology Skills
- saving work
- capturing and importing
- working with titles
- working with clips
- working in Storyboard View or Clip Viewer

Materials
- digital camera
- video camera

Teacher Preparation

1. Use the step-by-step directions included at the beginning of this book to teach students any necessary technology skills that they may not be familiar with.
2. Read the *Using Video Effects* step-by-step directions (page 27; page027.pdf).
3. Bookmark Internet sites that are appropriate for students so they can perform further research.
4. Remind students to bring their storyboards to class.

Procedure

1. Remind students of the previous lesson about the environment (*The Ecosystem—HELP!*). This lesson is a continuation of that lesson.
2. Have students capture and import any material they have to date.
3. Give students time to review their storyboards. Have them update these, if necessary, to include any new information.
4. Explain to students that, in this lesson, they are going to learn how to work with video effects. Video effects let you add special effects to your movie. There are 23–28 video effects to choose from. Tell the students that video effects should be used sparingly. Remind them that the focus should be on the content and not on the effects. However, when used appropriately, video effects can add to and support the content.

Procedure *(cont.)*

5. Have students experiment with different special effects on the scenes they have captured and imported. Explain to them that some effects may work great while others will not work at all. Remind them to be careful that the special effects they choose do not take away from the focus of their commercials.

6. Have students begin to add titles and credits to their storyboards.

7. Remind students that they should continue to research their chosen ideas. The more material they have to work with, the more editing choices they will have. It is better to have too many choices than not enough.

8. Tell students that for the next lesson they will be learning how to record narration while in Timeline View(er). In order to record narration, they will need scripts. So, between now and the next lesson, they should each write a script to record. Give them time to write and revise these scripts.

9. Review the rubric (page 196) so that students understand how their work will be assessed.

Extension Idea

Have students complete similar commercials by using special effects to visually tell stories about our ecosystem in the future.

Student Directions *Movie Maker*

1. Click **Collections**.
2. Click the ***Video Effect*** folder in the Collections pane.
3. Double-click the video effect you want to preview.
4. The video effect is previewed in the Monitor pane.
5. When you see one that you like, click on it. Hold down your mouse button and drag the desired effect to your chosen clip in the Storyboard or Timeline.
6. The effects icon star on the clip turns from gray to blue. That means the effect has been added.
7. If you want to delete an effect after you apply it, you can. On the clip with the effect that you want to delete, right-click the Effect icon in the lower-left corner.
8. Click **Delete Effects**.
9. The star turns from blue to gray and indicates that the video effect has been deleted.
10. Save your work.

Assessment Rubric

Strong (3 points)	Student experimented with at least four video effects. Effects chosen supported the concept.	Storyboard is complete and shows great detail. Titles are used and are pertinent to the concept.	Student's work shows a strong understanding of the lesson objectives.
Effective (2 points)	Student experimented with three video effects. Effects chosen supported the concept.	Storyboard is complete but could include more detail. A title is chosen for the movie, but few titles are used throughout.	Student's work shows an understanding of the lesson objectives.
Emerging (1 point)	Student experimented with two video effects. Video effects somewhat supported the concept.	Storyboard is complete but includes little detail. Title is chosen for the movie. No additional titles were chosen.	Student's work shows an emerging understanding of the lesson objectives.
Not Yet (0 points)	Student experimented with one video effect. Video effect did not support the content.	Storyboard is incomplete and shows no detail. No titles were chosen for the movie.	Student's work shows a weak understanding of the lesson objectives.
Self Score			
Teacher Score			
Total Score			
Comments			

The Ecosystem Speaks

Lesson Description

Students will record narration while in Timeline View or Timeline Viewer.

Content Standard

Students will know factors that affect the number and types of organisms an ecosystem can support (e.g., available resources; disease; competition from other organisms; predation).

Technology Skill

Students record narration for movies.

Additional Technology Skills

- saving work
- capturing and importing
- working with titles
- working with clips
- working in Timeline View or Timeline Viewer
- using video effects

Materials

- digital camera
- video camera

Teacher Preparation

1. Use the step-by-step directions included at the beginning of this book to teach students any necessary technology skills that they may not be familiar with.
2. Read the *Recording Narration* step-by-step directions (page 28; page028.pdf).
3. Remind students to bring in the scripts that they wrote.

Procedure

1. Remind students of the previous lessons about the environment (*The Ecosystem—HELP!* and *The Ecosystem in 30 Seconds*). This lesson is a continuation of those lessons.
2. Have students review their final scripts, reading them a few times to see if there is any room for improvement.
3. Explain to students that in this lesson they will learn how to record the scripts that they have created. If the students would like, they can act like directors. To do this, have them choose classmates to be the voice-overs for their commercials. If they prefer to be the voice-over, they should have classmates help with the recording.
4. Model for students how to use Timeline View(er) to record their narrations.

Procedure *(cont.)*

5. Give students time to record their narrations. If time permits, have them complete one or two takes. If possible, be aware of the timing of the scripts and make sure they do not get too long or too short.

6. After recording, have students see how the words fit with the pictures while in Timeline View(er). They may need to space some words out, cut a word or two, or add some more pictures. All of this is part of the editing process.

7. Give students time to capture and import any new video or stills they have to date.

8. Have students update their storyboards to include any new images or titles. Remind students that keeping their storyboards current will help them stay organized.

9. Review the rubric (page 200) so that students understand how their work will be assessed.

10. Tell students that for the next lesson they will continue to learn how to work with audio tracks. They will learn how to balance the audio between the audio and music tracks. These tracks include narration, audio from video clips, and music. Tell the students that they will need to have a selection of music for the next lesson.

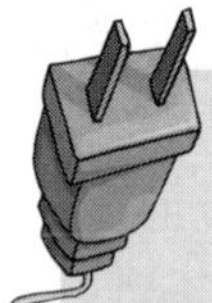

Extension Idea

Have students separate into groups and make lists of celebrities who they think have good voices and would sound interesting in their commercials. Aside from sounding good, advertisers use celebrities in their commercials because of their believability and credibility. Have the groups share their ideas.

Student Directions *Movie Maker*

1. In Timeline View, drag the Playhead to the location where you want to start the narration.

2. Click **Narrate Timeline**.

3. In the Narrate Timeline dialog box, adjust the Input level. As you speak, your voice should fall into the green area and rarely or never go into the red.

4. Click ***Start Narration*** and begin speaking. *Movie Maker* plays the video while you record, allowing you to time your narration to the movie.

5. Click ***Stop Narration***.

6. Enter a filename for your narration. *Movie Maker* automatically saves the narration into a folder called *Narration*, located in the *My Videos* folder with the rest of your clips.

7. Click **Save**.

8. Your narration appears in the Timeline, beginning at the location you specified in step 1.

Assessment Rubric

Strong (3 points)	Script completely explains the topic.	Student updated storyboard by including new video and audio.	Student successfully recorded the narration.	Student's work shows a strong understanding of the lesson objectives.
Effective (2 points)	Script generally explains the topic.	Student updated storyboard by including almost all of the new video and audio.	Student successfully recorded the narration, but some of the words are not clear.	Student's work shows an understanding of the lesson objectives.
Emerging (1 point)	Script attempts to explain the topic.	Student did not completely update storyboard.	Student recorded the narration with a lot of help.	Student's work shows an emerging understanding of the lesson objectives.
Not Yet (0 points)	Script does not explain the topic.	Student did not update storyboard.	Student did not successfully record the narration.	Student's work shows a weak understanding of the lesson objectives.
Self Score				
Teacher Score				
Total Score				

Comments

Sounds of the Ecosystem

Lesson Description

Students will learn how to adjust audio tracks while in Timeline View or Timeline Viewer. The audio tracks include narration tracks as well as the audio from any video clips they have imported.

Content Standard

Students will know factors that affect the number and types of organisms an ecosystem can support (e.g., available resources; disease; competition from other organisms; predation).

Technology Skill

Students adjust the audio balance between the audio and the audio music tracks.

Additional Technology Skills

- saving work
- capturing and importing video or audio
- using Timeline View or Timeline Viewer

Materials

- digital camera
- video camera
- CDs or iTunes song lists containing their music choices

Teacher Preparation

1. Use the step-by-step directions included at the beginning of this book to teach students any necessary technology skills that they may not be familiar with.

2. Read the *Adjusting Audio Balance* step-by-step directions (page 29; page029.pdf).

3. Make sure students have had a chance to gather some music together. Help them find music if they have not done so already.

Procedure

1. Remind students of the previous lessons about the environment (*The Ecosystem—HELP*, *The Ecosystem in 30 Seconds*, and *The Ecosystem Speaks*). This lesson is a continuation of those lessons.

2. Explain to students that in this lesson they will be learning how to balance the audio tracks in their commercials. The audio tracks consist of music, voice-over narration, and any audio associated with the video. Tell students to be careful that the music level does not overpower the level of the voice-over narration or audio from the video clips, as it is important to hear what is being said. If there is a break in the audio track, then the student can raise the volume of the music slightly to fill the hole.

3. For those who need it, model how to add audio from a CD or iTunes.

Procedure *(cont.)*

4. Ask students the following questions about the music they have chosen: *Do the music tracks support or enhance the content of the commercial? Do the songs move the story along? Is the music playing at the correct pace? Does it distract from the overall production?*

5. Have students import the music tracks they have selected.

6. Have students capture and import any new video they may have.

7. Demonstrate adjusting audio balance by following the step-by-step directions.

8. Give students time to work on their commercials by adjusting the balance of the audio tracks. Have them experiment with adjusting the volume. Tell them to play all of the tracks together at least three times to make sure all of the sound can be heard. If time permits, have them play their audio mixes (a *mix* is when all the audio tracks are adjusted and work together as the final track) for the class.

9. Remind students to save their work.

10. Tell students that in the next lesson they will be finishing their movies. This will be their last opportunity to add any video or make any changes.

11. Review the rubric (page 204) so that students will understand how their work will be assessed.

Extension Idea

Have students create similar commercials using only sound effects as their audio tracks. Students can make up their own sounds or download them from the Internet.

Student Directions *Movie Maker*

1. Right-click the audio clip that has a volume you want to change.
2. Choose **Volume** from the contextual menu.
3. Drag the slider to adjust the volume.
4. Select **OK**.
5. If you would rather use Audio Balance, click **Set Audio Levels** in the Timeline.
6. Drag the slider to adjust the audio balance. Dragging to the right will increase the Audio or Music volume level while decreasing the Audio from Video volume level. Dragging to the left will do the opposite.
7. When you are done, click the **X** in the upper right-hand corner of the box to close the Audio Levels dialog box.
8. If you want to mute the sound, right-click the audio clip for which you want to mute the volume.
9. Choose **Mute** from the contextual menu.
10. The sound is muted.

Assessment Rubric

Strong (3 points)	Music track enhances and supports the content of the commercial. The music is creative and interesting.	Student successfully balanced the audio tracks by making sure all the dialogue can be heard.	Student's work shows a strong understanding of the lesson objectives.
Effective (2 points)	Music track supports the content of the commercial.	Student balanced the audio tracks, but at times, the dialogue was difficult to hear.	Student's work shows an understanding of the lesson objectives.
Emerging (1 point)	Music track supports the content of the commercial, but it could be more interesting and less predictable.	Student somewhat balanced the audio tracks. The dialogue track was difficult to understand.	Students' work shows an emerging understanding of the lesson objectives.
Not Yet (0 points)	Music track does not support the content of the commercial, and is distracting at times.	Student did not balance the audio tracks.	Student's work shows a weak understanding of the lesson objectives.
Self Score			
Teacher Score			
Total Score			

Comments

The Ecosystem—The Final Spot

Lesson Description

Students will finish their commercials and learn how to save and share their commercials.

Content Standard

Students will know factors that affect the number and types of organisms an ecosystem can support (e.g., available resources; disease; competition from other organisms; predation).

Technology Skill

Students save and share their commercials on recordable CDs and as email attachments.

Additional Technology Skills

- saving work
- capturing and importing video or audio
- using Timeline View or Timeline Viewer
- working with AutoMovie or Magic iMovie

Materials

- digital camera
- video camera
- recordable CDs
- Internet access and email address from which to send emails

Teacher Preparation

1. Use the step-by-step directions included at the beginning of this book to teach students any necessary technology skills that they may not be familiar with.
2. Either have students bring in their own recordable CDs, or purchase some for the students.
3. Read the *Saving the Final Movie* step-by-step directions (page 31; page31.pdf).

Procedure

1. Remind students of the previous lessons about the environment (*The Ecosystem—HELP!*, *The Ecosystem in 30 Seconds*, *The Ecosystem Speaks*, and *Sounds of the Ecosystem*). This lesson is the culmination of those lessons.
2. Remind students about their work on movie making. In these lessons, they learned how to work with titles, clips, music, and audio. They learned how to record narration, balance audio tracks, and finish their movies using AutoMovie or Magic iMovie.
3. Explain to students that, in this lesson, they are going to complete their commercials using AutoMovie or Magic iMovie. Go over this technology, and make sure students are comfortable choosing styles or transitions.

Procedure (cont.)

4. Challenge students to see if they can make any improvements to the visuals first. Ask the following questions: *If titles are used, do they support the content of the commercial? Are they visually interesting, or could they use some improvement? Is the editing style chosen the best for the commercial? Are the transitions working?*
5. Have students move on to the audio parts of their commercials. Ask the following questions: *Is the dialogue clear? Can you understand every word that is being said? Does the music help or hurt the commercial? Does the narration support the content of the commercial?*
6. Give students time to work on and finish their commercials. Tell them to make at least one change that will improve their work.
7. Have students share their completed commercials with the class. After all the commercials have been shared, have students choose their favorite commercials. Have students offer one another some constructive criticism and praise.
8. Explain to students that they will now learn how to save and share their commercials on recordable CDs and as email attachments. Review the step-by-step directions on *Saving the Final Movie* (page 31; page031.pdf).
9. Give students time to share their work.
10. Review the rubric (page 208) so that students understand how their work will be assessed.

Extension Idea

Have students compare their finished commercials with favorite TV commercials. They can compare these commercials using Venn diagrams.

Student Directions *Movie Maker*

Saving Your Final Movie to a CD

1. Click **Tasks**.
2. Under Finish Movie, click ***Save to CD***.
3. In the Save Movie wizard, type a filename for your saved movie.
4. Type a name for the CD.
5. Click ***Next*** at the bottom of the window.
6. Click ***Next*** again.
7. Depending on the length of your movie, it might take several minutes to save.
8. If you want to save the movie to another CD, click the *Save the movie to another recordable CD* box.
9. Click **Finish**.
10. Your movie is saved.

Saving Your Final Movie As an Email Attachment

1. Click **Tasks**.
2. Under Finish Movie, click ***Send in email***.
3. Depending on the length of your movie, it might take a few minutes to save.
4. If you want to save a copy of the movie on your computer, click *Save a copy of the movie on my computer*.
5. Select *Next* at the bottom of the window.
6. Your email application opens, and a new email is created with the movie attached.
7. Type in an email address and a message.
8. Click **Send**.

Assessment Rubric

Strong (3 points)	Movie is at least 20–30 seconds long.	Movie is visually appealing, and the titles improve the presentation.	Audio tracks are well balanced and enhance the content of the movie.	Student's work shows a strong understanding of the lesson objectives.
Effective (2 points)	Movie is 15–19 seconds long.	Movie is visually appealing, and titles were used.	Audio tracks are balanced and somewhat enhance the content of the movie.	Student's work shows an understanding of the lesson objectives.
Emerging (1 point)	Movie is between 10–14 seconds long.	Movie is somewhat visually appealing, and titles are used inconsistently.	Audio tracks are balanced but at times do not support the content of the movie.	Student's work shows an emerging understanding of the lesson objectives.
Not Yet (0 points)	Movie is less than 10 seconds long.	Movie is visually unappealing, and no titles were used.	Audio tracks are not well balanced and do not support the content of the movie.	Student's work shows a weak understanding of the lesson objectives.
Self Score				
Teacher Score				
Total Score				
Comments				

Table of Contents

Works Cited

Britt, Judy, Joe P. Brasher, and Lydia D. Davenport. 2007. Balancing books & bytes. *Kappa Delta Pi*, 43: 122–127.

Eisenberg, Michael B., and Doug Johnson. 1996. Computer skills for information problem solving: Learning and teaching technology in context. *Emergency Librarian*.

Mitchell, Karen, Marianne Bakia, and Edith Yang. 2007. State strategies and practices for educational technology: Volume II—Supporting mathematics instruction with educational technology. Washington, DC: U.S. Department of Education, Office of Planning, Evaluation, and Policy Development.

Valdez, Gilbert, Mary McNabb, May Foertsch, May Anderson, Mark Hawkdes, and Lenaya Raack. 1999. Computer-based technology and learning: Evolving uses and expectations. North Central Regional Educational Laboratory.

White, Noel, Cathy Ringstaff, and Loretta Kelley. 2002. *Getting the most from technology in schools*. San Francisco, CA: WestEd.

Other References

4Teachers. Project based learning checklists. http://pblchecklist.4teachers.org/checklist.shtml (accessed 5/14/07).

The George Lucas Educational Foundation. Why is problem-based learning important? http://www.edutopia.org/modules/PBL/whypbl.php (accessed 1/14/07).

Contents of Teacher Resource CD

Student Samples

The following movie sample files include both *.avi* and *.mov* files. The *.avi* files are to be used with Windows platforms and the *.mov* files are to be used with Macintosh platforms.

Page	Lesson Title	Sample Title	Filename
32	Patterns Everywhere!	K–2 pattern images	stripes.jpg; argyle.jpg; checkerboard; jpg
36	Patterns That Move	K–2 patterns clips	pattern01_clip.avi; pattern01_clip.mov
40	Working with Patterns	K–2 patterns clips in order	pattern01_ordr.avi; pattern01_ordr.mov
44	Patterns, Patterns, Patterns	K–2 patterns clips with titles and credits	pattern01_crdts.avi; pattern01_crdts.mov
48	Patterns—The Movie!	K–2 patterns movie	pattern01_movie.avi; pattern01_movie.mov
92	Linear Patterns	3–5 pattern images	quilt.jpg; argyle.jpg; stripes; jpg
96	Growing Patterns	3–5 patterns clips	pattern02_clip.avi; pattern02_clip.mov
100	Repeating Patterns	3–5 patterns clips in order	pattern02_ordr.avi; pattern02_ordr.mov
104	Giving Patterns Titles	3–5 patterns clips with titles and credits	pattern02_crdts.avi; pattern02_crdts.mov
108	Patterns Around Us Movie	3–5 patterns movie	pattern02_movie.avi; pattern02_movie.mov
153	Fibonacci Pattern Clips	6–8 patterns clips	pattern03_clip.avi; pattern03_clip.mov
158	Fibonacci Sequences	6–8 patterns clips in order	pattern03_ordr.avi; pattern03_ordr.mov
162	Giving Titles to Fibonacci Sequences	6–8 patterns clips with titles and credits	pattern03_crdts.avi; pattern03_crdts.mov
166	Fibonacci Patterns Movie	6–8 patterns movie	pattern03_movie.avi; pattern03_movie.mov

Student Templates

Title	Filename
K–2 storyboard template	storyboard01.doc
3–5 storyboard template	storyboard02.doc
6–8 storyboard template	storyboard03.doc
Shot list template	shotlist.doc

Teacher Resources

Title	Filename
Blank rubric	rubric.pdf
Learn and Use Series Description	series.pdf

Contents of Teacher Resource CD *(cont.)*

Step-by-Step Directions Pages for PC Users

Page	Title	Filename
14	Starting and Saving Projects	page014.pdf; vista014.pdf
15	Capturing and Importing Images	page015.pdf; vista015.pdf
16	Working with Clips	page016.pdf; vista016.pdf
17	Working in Storyboard View	page017.pdf; vista017.pdf
18	Adding Titles and Credits	page018.pdf vista018.pdf
19	Using AutoMovie	page019.pdf; vista019.pdf
20	Adding Titles Before and After a Clip	page020.pdf; vista020.pdf
21	Working with Audio	page021.pdf; vista021.pdf
23	Working with Music	page023.pdf; vista023.pdf
24	Rearranging Clip Sequences and Deleting Clips	page024.pdf; vista024.pdf
25	Selecting a Movie Style	page025.pdf; vista025.pdf
26	Filming Techniques	page026.pdf
27	Using Video Effects	page027.pdf vista027.pdf
28	Recording Narration	page028.pdf; vista028.pdf
29	Adjusting Audio Balance	page029.pdf; vista029.pdf
30	Producing the Movie	page030.pdf; vista030.pdf
31	Saving the Final Movie	page031.pdf; vista031.pdf

Step-by-Step Directions Pages for Macintosh Users

Page	Title	Filename
14	Starting and Saving Projects	mac014.pdf
15	Capturing and Importing Images	mac015.pdf
16	Working with Clips	mac016.pdf
17	Working with Clip Viewer	mac017.pdf
18	Adding Titles and Credits	mac018.pdf
19	Using Magic iMovie	mac019.pdf
20	Adding Titles Before and After a Clip	mac020.pdf
21	Working with Audio	mac021.pdf
23	Working with Music	mac023.pdf
24	Rearranging Clip Sequences and Deleting Clips	mac024.pdf
25	Selecting an iMovie Style	mac025.pdf
27	Using Video Effects	mac027.pdf
28	Recording Narration	mac028.pdf
29	Adjusting Audio Balance	mac029.pdf
30	Producing the Movie	mac030.pdf
31	Saving the Final Movie	mac031.pdf

Assessment Rubric

Strong (3 points)	Movie shows at least 12 photographs and/or video clips.	Movie is visually appealing, and the titles improve the presentation.	Transitions enhance the content of the movie.	Student's work shows a strong understanding of the lesson objectives.
Effective (2 points)	Movie shows 9–11 photographs and/or video clips.	Movie is visually appealing, and titles were used.	Transitions somewhat enhance the content of the movie.	Student's work shows an understanding of the lesson objectives.
Emerging (1 point)	Movie shows 6–8 photographs and/or video clips.	Movie is somewhat visually appealing.	Some of the transitions enhance the content of the movie, while a few of them detract from it.	Student's work shows an emerging understanding of the lesson objectives.
Not Yet (0 points)	Movie shows at least five photographs and/or movie clips.	Movie is visually unappealing, and no titles were used.	Transitions detract from the overall flow of the movie.	Student's work shows a weak understanding of the lesson objectives.
Self Score				
Teacher Score				
Total Score				
Comments				

Procedure *(cont.)*

3. Tell students that they will be making television commercials about simple things that they can do in their everyday lives to benefit the ecosystem. The commercial should be 30 seconds long.

4. Review the phrases on the board. Ask the class to think about what these phrases have to do with the ecosystem. Brainstorm with the class some possible ideas for their commercials, using the phrases on the board as topics. An idea for a commercial titled "Parties" could be the following scenario: We see a party taking place and notice that there are no paper plates, napkins, or plastic anywhere. The packages we see are wrapped in brown paper, and the ribbon and cards are all reused from previous gifts. For gifts, we see a shot of the "gift of giving", like babysitting or lawn mowing, instead of material gifts.

5. Distribute copies of the 6–8 storyboard template (storyboard03.doc). and copies of *Filming Techniques* (page 26).

6. As an exercise, have students again review the commercials you brought. They should each pick one and do a storyboard for that commercial. Have them examine what types of shots are in the commercial (close-up shots, wide shots, long shots, pans, or zooms). They should make note of these on their storyboards. Other things to describe in the storyboards are actors, props, different locations, notes on dialog, and voice-over narration. Remind them to add titles to their storyboard frames when titles are used.

7. Remind students that when there is music throughout the commercial, they should indicate this at the beginning of their storyboards using the words *music throughout*.

8. Now have students review their storyboards by comparing them to the finished commercial examples.

9. Have students start to work on their storyboards for their own commercials. Explain that they will be working on this commercial for a few lessons so their storyboards will be continually updated as they gather more materials.

10. Tell students to continue to work on their projects by keeping in mind how to shoot the different camera angles, movements, and shots.

11. Review the rubric (page 192) so that students will see how their work will be assessed.

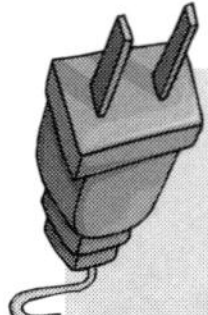

Extension Idea

Sometimes using still photographs and titles are very powerful. Have the students create commercials using only still photographs, titles, and music to tell their stories.

Contents of Teacher Resource CD *(cont.)*

Student Directions Pages for Macintosh Users *(cont.)*

Page	Title	Filename
145	Our Environment—Mixing Elements	mac175.pdf
149	Our Environment—The Finished Commercial	mac149.pdf
155	Fibonacci Pattern Clips	mac155.pdf
160	Fibonacci Sequences	mac160.pdf
164	Giving Titles to Fibonacci Sequences	mac164.pdf
168	Fibonacci Patterns Movies	mac168.pdf
172	Historical Figures	mac172.pdf
176	Historical Figures on a Timeline	mac176.pdf
180	Making Music Work	mac180.pdf
184	Sequencing the Movie	mac184.pdf
188	Historical Figures—The Video	mac188.pdf
195	The Ecosystem in 30 Seconds	mac195.pdf
199	The Ecosystem Speaks	mac199.pdf
203	Sounds of the Ecosystem	mac203.pdf
207	The Ecosystem—The Final Spot	mac207.pdf

Notes